M000315516

50 Ways to Cook a Carrot

50 Ways to Cook a Carrot

Peter Hertzmann

PROSPECT BOOKS

2019

First published in 2019 in Great Britain and the United States
by Prospect Books, 26 Parke Road, London, SW13 9NG.

Text and photographs ©2019 Peter Hertzmann.

The author, Peter Hertzmann, asserts his right to be identified as author of
this work in accordance with the Copyright, Designs & Patents Act 1988.

No part of this publication may be reproduced, stored in a retrieval
system, or transmitted in any form or by any means, electronic, mechanical,
photocopying, recording or otherwise, without the prior permission of
the copyright holder.

BRITISH LIBRARY CATALOGUING IN PUBLICATION DATA:
A catalogue entry of this book is available from the British Library.

Typeset and designed by Brendan King and Catheryn Kilgarriff in Gill Sans
Nova and Garamond Premier Pro.

ISBN 978-1-909248-63-2

Printed and bound by the Gutenberg Press, Malta.

Contents

Savoury Cooked Methods Served Hot

Sweet Cooked Methods Served Cold

Methods for Prepared Ingredients

Author's Note

Because this book is designed to teach methods and not simply be a book of recipes, it is impractical to organize as is normal for a cookbook. Yes, there are both sweet and savoury items, but there are also items meant to be no more than ingredients in other dishes. Even the divisions that I've chosen are somewhat artificial, and some methods fit into more than one group.

Notes on Units of Measure

Throughout the methods detailed in this book, measurements are provided in metric units followed by their U.S. equivalents in round brackets (parenthesis in the U.S.). For example, 250 ml may be expressed as 1 cup (meaning 1 U.S. cup) where exact equivalence is not important. It may also be expressed as 8½ fl oz (meaning 8½ U.S. fluid ounces) where equivalence is more important. There is a difference between the customary U.S. cup used here (237 ml) and the legal U.S. cup (240 ml), the metric cup (250 ml), and the Japanese cup (200 ml).

All the recipes were written and tested using metric units. The U.S. equivalents shown are calculated and have not been tested.

The size of the eggs used throughout this book is 'large'. One 'large' British egg is roughly equivalent to one 'extra-large' U.S. egg.

Notes on Terminology

Oscar Wilde wrote, 'we have really everything in common with America nowadays, except, of course, language.' When it comes to kitchen terminology, not much has changed in the intervening 130 years.

U.K. Term	U.S. Equivalent
sultana	raisin
courgette	zucchini or Italian squash
wholemeal	whole wheat
spirit vinegar	distilled vinegar
biscuits	cookies
mash	purée
plain flour	all-purpose flour
strong flour	bread flour
double cream	manufacturer's cream (use heavy cream if higher butterfat cream is unavailable)
icing sugar	powdered sugar
caster sugar	superfine sugar
jelly	jello (when referring to a gelatine dessert)
cornflour	cornstarch
greaseproof paper	parchment paper or pan liner
cling film	plastic wrap
kitchen paper	paper towels
tea towel	dish towel
elastic band	rubber band
hob	burner (as on a stove or range)
liquidiser	blender
allotment	a plot of public land rented by an individual for growing vegetables or flowers
jumble sale	rummage sale

Introduction

In 1974, I purchased a rather thick book about Chinese cookery that claimed to contain over a thousand recipes. I thought I could teach myself to cook Chinese food from this handsome book. Fortunately, after a few stumbles, I met a recent Taiwanese immigrant. She taught me the basic methods of Chinese cooking and introduced me to a couple of sources for the ingredients. I was on my way. Learning the methods of Chinese cooking set me on the right path.

Twenty years later, I was perusing a copy of *Fine Cooking Magazine* at a newsstand. There I found an article titled, 'Two Steps to Moist Pork Chops'. The article was touting the 'sear, roast, rest' method common to many restaurants. Although the text only mentioned pork chops, I found that I could apply the method successfully to almost any meat or seafood. In the process, I managed to translate a single recipe into a generalized method. Once again, learning a method helped to free me from being a follower of recipes.

I spent thirty days in 2000 in a small village in the Jura. It was so small that the village cows far outnumbered the village inhabitants. At the edge of the village lay Le Château d'Amondans, then a Michelin one-star restaurant and hotel established in a 250-year-old mansion. I was there for my first *stage*, an activity that resembles an unpaid internship. It is common for newly trained cooks to *stage* in several restaurants in order to learn different skills and to pad their résumés. I was totally untrained and 52 years old. I was older than everyone working in the restaurant except for the chef's father-in-law. At the end of my period as a *stagiaire*, I had a passel of new recipes under my arm, but more importantly, I had learned what has become a lifetime of cooking methods which continue to guide me.

I could now hold food for hours after cooking and still serve it hot and in perfect form. I could now prepare food in simple ways that seemed complex to the diner. I could now prepare a banquet for a large group without breaking a sweat.

Over the next seven or eight years, I *staged* as often as three times a year in restaurants in France, Switzerland, Canada, and the United States. Each time I learned new methods to add to my kit.

In 2015, I visited the chef from Amondans who now was operating a small restaurant in the Swiss Alps. This restaurant was much smaller than his original Michelin-starred restaurant, and his clientele favoured traditional Swiss snacks rather than French haute cuisine. For the chef's sanity, the menu also included a few gastronomic dishes from the French lexicon. I visited the chef for a week. I joined him in the kitchen, and for a week we cooked up a storm. I was able to contribute and participate with a minimum of instruction. Even though I had never cooked any of the dishes I was now pushing through the pass, we were like a young couple dancing as a well-practised pair.

The following year, I spent a month at an experimental restaurant in Scotland. There were only four workers in the entire restaurant. We did everything from cooking to serving to cleaning. Each of the four days the restaurant served dinner, we gathered at ten in the morning and began to plan the evening meal. The menu evolved during the day. Sometimes it even changed during service. At eight each night, up to thirty guests were served a seven-course dinner that included house-made bread. Each night's dinner was unique. Some nights were better than others, but no night was mediocre. What made each night possible was that all of us in the kitchen knew how to cook. We never worked from recipes, we just cooked. How could this be? We all were well-versed in the 'methods' of cooking.

My belief in teaching the methods of cooking, rather than recipes, started to come to fruition in 2008 when I was teaching part-time in a job training centre set up to provide people with no job experience the skills required for entry-level positions. I had a group of culinary students who, besides being new to the programme, were mostly residents of the county jail. They attended class each day as part of a work furlough programme. Each night, they were back in jail.

When I arrived one morning, the chef assigned a new group to my tutelage. In thirty days, the group was supposed to compete in a cooking contest against a group of students from a local junior college who were three-quarters through a professional, two-year programme. The morning of the contest, they were to be given a market basket of food, and they had three hours to produce some number of dishes. I decided to teach as many generalized methods of cooking as I could during the time I had to spend with them. In the end, none of our groups finished first, but all performed better than most of the college-trained students.

In 1993, Fuji television brought the world the archetype of all modern cooking competitions on television, *Iron Chef*. The timed cooking 'battle' had the competitors producing dishes around a theme ingredient. The end product was the direct result of the cooks applying cooking methods from their experience to the competition.

In contrast, during the ten years I taught recreational cooking at a large, nationwide cookware store, I was constantly confronted by students who came to learn specific recipes rather than those who wanted to learn to cook. For example, rather than learn the methods required to produce almost all soups, some students only wanted to learn how to make a specific soup. Many even closed their ears to possible substitutions which allowed each student to expand his — men were more of a problem — repertoire.

By now, you are aware that I push methods over individual recipes. Escoffier gives a recipe for 'purée de céleri' in his *Guide Culinaire*. The method in the recipe produces a soup that diners swear contains cream, but it doesn't. I have substituted many different vegetables for the celery in the recipe, and the results are equally good. The one constant is that the method to produce the soup is the same in all cases.

Part of my goal in teaching methods rather than recipes is to eliminate the inherent variances between different cooking environments. My stove is different than yours. My pots, tools, and work area are different than yours. My selection and sources of ingredients are different than yours. If I provide unique recipes, they may or may not work as prescribed in your kitchen because of all these differences, but if I provide you with the methods of cooking, the preparation of dishes becomes easy and repeatable.

To further simplify my argument, all the methods are applied to a single ingredient: carrots. Why carrots? They are versatile. They are readily available. They are cheap. Although each method presented results in a usable carrot preparation, the carrot is really a stand-in for many other possible ingredients. This is important to remember: Although we'll make pastry cream from carrots, there are many, many ingredients that could be used exactly the same as carrots (including the original milk).

Every method presented in this book is approachable for both novice cooks and those with many years' experience. Although some prescriptive advice is provided – such as when the salt concentration for pickling a carrot is given as a certain percent – this type of information is only provided when necessary. In this manner, we can concentrate on the method of preparation and not on any one recipe. In this way, the method can be applied to hundreds of ingredients, not just carrots.

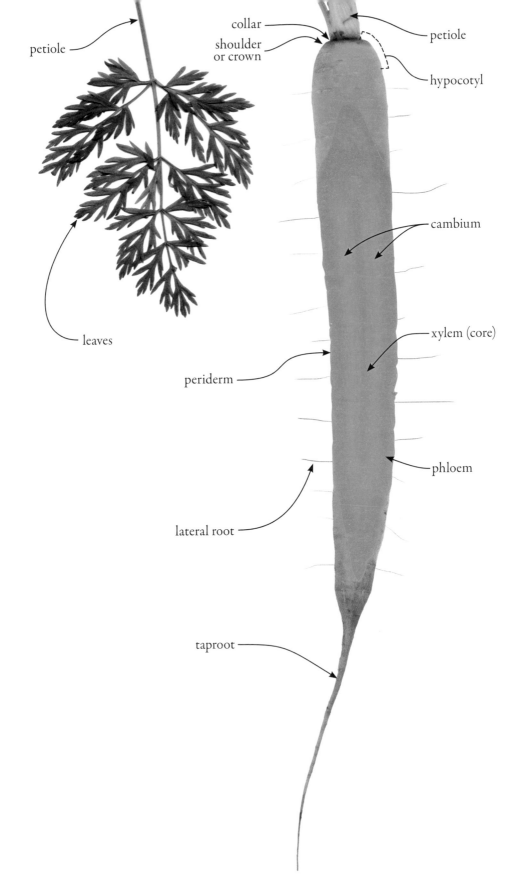

petiole

collar

shoulder
or crown

petiole

hypocotyl

cambium

xylem (core)

periderm

phloem

leaves

lateral root

phloem

taproot

General Information

Even though this is a book about cooking, not about carrots – the carrot is a stand-in for other foods that could be treated in a similar fashion – it is important to understand our star ingredient. We need to understand how it is composed. For example, does the juice have enough starch to thicken on its own when heated? How much pectin – a common polysaccharide that helps an ingredient to gel – does it contain? That can affect how we use it. We also need to understand how to buy carrots and prepare them for use in the various concoctions that we dream up.

Parts of a carrot

Most of the time when we buy a carrot, we are buying only the storage root of the vegetable. As in most vegetables, there's more to the carrot than what we see at first glance. When carrots grow in the earth, only a small portion of the part we commonly call a carrot is visible above the surface of the soil. Most of the carrot is buried. The buried part is the storage root and the visible part is called the hypocotyl. The top of the hypocotyl, where the carrot surface rounds towards the stalks, is the shoulder or crown. Where the stalks meet the root is a groove called the collar. The collar can be very slight or very pronounced. The little hairy roots emanating from the sides of the storage root are called lateral roots, and the root at the tip of the carrot is the taproot. The botanical term for the stalks is the petiole. There may be a remnant of the petiole still attached to the carrot if, like most shoppers, you purchase carrots without their greens attached. The carrot doesn't have a truly separate skin. When we pare or scrape a carrot, we are removing the periderm. The periderm is simply the outer edge or surface of the phloem. The phloem is the body – I haven't found a generic name for this part of the carrot, so I've chosen body – but doesn't include the xylem, or core. The core is considered the woody portion of the storage root, but both it and the phloem are the vascular tissue that conducts sugars and other metabolic products downward from the leaves. Between the xylem and the phloem is a layer called the cambium. It is from this thin layer that the two vascular portions grow.

The petiole, or the stalks, terminate in the leaves. If left in the ground for two seasons, a central stalk grows from the crown and a flower grows at its tip. Since the flower doesn't make an appearance until the second year, it rarely shows up in markets. I assume that it is edible, but I have never found one to try. The individual clusters of tiny flowers make a nice decoration, but I've only seen them in pictures on the internet.

The portion of the carrot's anatomy that interests most people is the storage root. In some carrots, the core of the root can be quite woody and bitter compared to the remainder of the carrot. Some recipes call for removing and discarding the core. I guess that I'm lucky. The core hasn't been a problem for me, so I don't remove it. Maybe it's just not a problem with our modern, hybridized carrots, but there may still be an issue with carrots grown from heirloom seeds.

Those are all the 'big' parts of carrots. As in all food, there's a bunch of 'little' parts, too. The small part we hear most about is beta-carotene. Beta-carotene is a pigment molecule that your body converts to Vitamin A. I have not found a dietary standard for beta-carotene, but there is one for Vitamin A. According to several studies I've read, we need to eat about 25 to 80 grams (1 to 3 ounces) of raw carrot each day to fulfil all of our Vitamin A needs. Apparently, your body only converts as much beta-carotene into Vitamin A as you need. High doses of beta-carotene can be toxic, but the amount seems much, much higher than a normal person eats in their normal diet.

The other small parts of carrots we are interested in is the water, starch, pectin, and sugar. Knowledge of the specific amounts present of each of these components can help us develop the fifty different ways to cook carrots. Knowing that the storage root is about 88% water helps us predict the yield from a given amount of carrots when we juice them, since juicers tend to be about 50% efficient. Based on these two percentages, a kilogram (2¼ pounds) of carrots yields about 450 millilitres (15 fluid ounces) of raw juice.

Knowing that there is about 1.5% starch in an average carrot — a russet potato is about 17% starch — tells us that the binding capability of the raw storage root is low, and that a raw carrot is not be an effective way to thicken a sauce. If we dry the carrot, the starch content increases to about 12%, which is a significant boost in its ability to gel a liquid, but not competitive with common starches, such as cornflour.

Carrots have one of the highest levels of pectin found in any vegetable. This means that carrots should gel rather easily if treated properly with heat or tannins. The nearly 5% sugar in carrots means that everything we produce has the potential to be naturally sweet.

How did I determine the basic information in the previous paragraph? The United States Department of Agriculture maintains an online *National Nutrient Database for Standard Reference*. I just searched on the internet for that phrase and clicked on the first result. This led me to a page with the expression 'Start your search here' prominently displayed in the centre. The words were like a big button urging me to click. So I did. From there, it became just a matter of typing 'carrots, raw' in the search box, and then selecting the same from the list that popped up. You can easily do a nutrient search of over 8,000 food items in the database – in other words, you can figure out the potential capabilities of nearly anything you'd ever put in your pantry or refrigerator.

Purchasing carrots

The form you buy your carrots in is partially a function of where you live and where you shop. If I go to one of my local super-sized, conventional markets, I can find both organic and conventional carrots loose and in many packaging schemes from half-kilo (one-pound) to five-kilo (ten-pound) bags labelled 'for juicing'. The smaller-quantity bags even allow the buyer to observe a little of the product inside, but it's obviously only meant as a teaser. The last time I looked, I counted twelve different combinations of carrot types and quantities on the shelves, without considering the variations of the baby-cut carrots. There were a few organic carrots available loose, but these did not occupy anywhere near the shelf space of the packaged carrots. There were also true baby carrots available in orange, white, and purple sold with their greens attached, but only in very small quantities. These carrots were an exception since most of those available were orange and without their greens. My unverified perception is that the average shopper at the store perceives bagged carrots as being more desirable.

The organic vegetable stores nearby tend to emphasize loose carrots over their packaged cousins. They still have at least one choice – usually a house brand – of the bagged baby-cut carrots. In contrast, the ethnic stores in my neighbourhood almost universally only sell loose carrots. All these places still only sell the carrots without the greens.

Buying carrots at my local farmers market affords the only opportunity I have to buy the carrots with their greens still attached. I've noticed that great-looking carrots are often sold with pitiful greens, and great-looking greens often seem to be attached to sorrowful carrots. I've also noticed that many shoppers only want to buy carrots with the greens still attached, but while completing their transaction, they ask the vendor to rip off and discard the greens. I can only assume that they think that carrots with the greens still attached are fresher or tastier.

Unfortunately, in my county, the public health officials consider the greens removed from the carrots to be contaminated waste and prevent the vendors from selling the greens separately, or even giving them away for free. There is an exception if the greens are for your rabbits or chickens. I recently adopted a six-foot tall rabbit named Harvey who makes it possible for me to stock up on free greens every time I'm at the market. I'm waiting for the day they ask to see his picture.

Storing carrots

When properly stored, carrots, like most root vegetables, can last almost a year, or until the next crop is ready. This, of course, assumes that the grower is only growing one carrot crop a year. The carrots' condition at the end of the storage period is a large variable. It doesn't necessarily mean that elderly carrots are inedible. It just means that they must be used in an appropriate manner, and other parts of the preparation may require adjustment to accommodate the carrots' special needs. The specimens available from my supermarket in the middle of winter are often a bit old, or in possession of a generous share of frequent flyer mileage, probably because they have been stored already bagged. For long-term storage, carrots have traditionally been stored buried in sawdust at root-cellar temperature, but that method is not available for commercial storage.

For home use, we normally just store the carrots in our refrigerator. In my refrigerator, that means I have many weeks before the carrots start becoming limp. Luckily, I can buy fresh carrots all-year-round. Long-term storage is not an issue for me. But what about your refrigerator? Modern refrigerators, as in those built since 1949 when the major manufacturers patented several methods to eliminate frost build-up, use various means to reduce the humidity in the refrigerator compartment. Therefore, food dries out if not wrapped properly. Many modern refrigerators have separate vegetable compartments with rubber seals to separate them from the main part of the refrigerator. The seals also prevent the refrigerator's dehumidification mechanism from drying out the contents. I have good luck with storing unwrapped carrots in this type of compartment.

If you purchase bagged carrots, look at the bag carefully. Many have small holes in the plastic so the carrots don't sit in moisture and potentially rot sooner. Packaged this way, carrots last longer in the main part of your refrigerator than if they weren't bagged at all, but they last better unwrapped in a sealed vegetable compartment.

Unfortunately, even though I am close to two, year-round farmers markets with growers who produce carrots year-round, the best carrot greens seem to be available during the summer months unless I custom order some a week in advance. Once I get them home, properly cleaned and dried of surface moisture, carrot greens last quite a few weeks in a closed container in a modern, low-humidity refrigerator. The moisture removal after washing is very important and is discussed in the next section.

Because of a lack of general availability, only one of the methods discussed later requires carrot greens. That doesn't mean you can't or shouldn't give a few a try if you find yourself awash in carrot greens.

Washing carrots

When and how to clean a carrot is a function of where you buy it and what condition you buy it in. If you pick up a bag of carrots at your local supermarket, the carrots are already clean of the dirt that clung to them when they were harvested. If the bag is dry on the outside – I've been in too many markets where they spray their bagged carrots – and the carrots aren't swimming in water on the inside, you can put off washing them until use. I treat loose carrots that I buy from the produce department of my local market the same way as bagged carrots. They just go loose into the vegetable compartment of my refrigerator.

Buying carrots from your farmers market can be a different story. They may be for sale loose without greens, loose with greens, bunched without greens, or bunched with greens. My experience with my local markets is that carrots sold without their greens have been washed by the vendor, and carrots sold with their greens have not been washed. I suggest handling any previously washed carrots the same as loose carrots from a grocery store.

The storage root and the greens of a carrot need to be washed separately. Let's look at the root first. Not all things black or brown on the carrot are dirt. Dirt may be attached to the overall surface, but the areas where the lateral roots were attached, or still are attached, and the groove that makes up the collar, may be dark and appear dirty. This is a discolouring of the surface of the root, not dirt. It does not wash off.

Start by soaking the carrot roots in a basin of cold tap water for five minutes or so. This should loosen up much of the true dirt. One by one, remove a carrot from your basin and brush off any remaining dirt, which now should be mud, with a stiff-bristle vegetable brush. When the batch of carrots are clean, rinse the basin and refill it with cold water. Return the carrots to the basin. Soak the carrots for another minute or so. One by one, remove each carrot and shake off the excess water. If they seem too wet after shaking, dry the carrots lightly with a tea towel. These shiny-clean carrots are now ready for you to use right away or store.

The carrot greens require a bit more work than the roots. Even those purchased still attached to previously washed carrots still need to be cleaned further. Start by separating the greens – leaving the leaves attached to their stems – into bunches that you can soak for about five minutes per batch. Carrots are often planted in sandy soil. The stalks are shaped like tiny celery stalks that capture the sand. When the greens are soaked long enough, remove the bunch, allow it to drain. Then spin the greens in batches in a salad spinner. Spin each batch twice to remove as much surface water as you can. Cover a standard, rimmed baking sheet or similar size tray with a clean tea towel. Tuck the edges of the towel in so they don't extend over the edge of my baking sheet. Cover the towel with a single layer of kitchen paper. Arrange the spin-dried greens on the prepared baking sheet so they are spread out as much as possible. Place the sheet in the main part of your refrigerator, assuming you have a modern, frost-free refrigerator. (If your refrigerator is not frost-free, this method does not work because it lacks a dehumidifier.) Leave the greens uncovered, or if you wish cover them with a single layer of kitchen paper. After a few hours the top part of the stack of greens is dry. Flip the stack to expose the remaining wet portion to the dry refrigerator air. In my refrigerator, this process usually happens overnight.

When dry, remove the tray of greens from your refrigerator and separate the leaves from the stems. This process, when done properly, can be time consuming and tedious. I usually do it in the morning after my second espresso. Except for the terminal leaf cluster – the one at the end – the leaves are arranged in one or more pairs along the stalk. Each pair tends to 'point' to one side of the stalk. Starting with the leaf-pair closest to the root-end of the stalk, bring your thumb and forefinger from the back side of the stalk to fold the pair of leaves in the direction they are naturally pointing, and leaving their short stems attached to the stalk, pick off just the leaves. Work your way up the stalk until just the terminal leaf cluster remains. Pick the three leaves of the cluster off the stem as a group. Their leaf stems are usually quite short and tender. Store the greens in a closed container as suggested above. I have found that plastic bags with the sliding, zipper-like closure work quite well. Press the bag slightly before closing the last little bit to expel most of the air captured in the bag. The stalks, if you are planning to save them for use, can be wrapped in plastic wrap for storage.

Paring carrots

The decision to pare a carrot – since carrots have no skin, they cannot be peeled – should be made based on how the carrot is to be used rather than habit. There is a strong tradition to always pare carrots. I believe this is because, in times past, carrots were sold dirty or even pulled from one's own allotment. Paring or scraping was an effective way of removing any dirt that wouldn't easily wash off. Today, the carrots you buy in most venues have been washed at least once before making their way to your shopping basket. I advise whether to pare carrots in each of the carrot-cooking methods that follow in this text. For those methods where paring is appropriate, the following may be helpful.

Starting in the late 1860s, there were guides patented that could be attached to a paring knife to limit the depth that a carrot, or any vegetable, could be pared or peeled. These guides were no longer necessary once fixed-space peelers were developed. The first modern peelers came into existence around the turn of the twentieth century – the earliest patent I have found is dated 1905. Today, there are two basic shapes to choose from: so-called yoke-peelers (or Y-peelers) and straight-peelers.

Prior to the common availability of effective peelers, carrots were usually scraped with the edge of a paring knife. As Fanny Merritt Farmer wrote in *The Boston Cooking-School Cook Book* in 1896: 'To prepare carrots for cooking, wash and scrape, as the best flavour and brightest colours are near the skin.' (No one told Farmer that carrots don't have skins!) By the time Irma Rombauer published *The Joy of Cooking* in 1931, peeling had mostly replaced scraping, although in one recipe she writes, 'Carrots may be boiled peeled, or unpeeled. [...] Wash and scrape carrots, or merely wash them.' In this one place where Rombauer mentions scraping, she implies that scraping is an alternative to washing, not to paring. Now, almost a century later, we can still scrape carrots as an alternative to washing, or even paring, but we must be aware that scraping can make a mess of our work area. I prefer washing and paring.

Straight-peelers have their blade parallel to the handle of the peeler. As originally designed, the blade is fixed. This style is still very common in France. The swivel-version of a straight-peeler allows the blade to easily sit in a proper cutting position. Y-peelers have their blade at a right angle to the handle. The blade in a Y-peeler always swivels.

The blades in both types of peelers may be made of carbon steel or stainless steel. Carbon-steel blades tend to be sharper and stay sharper for much longer. Because they are made from carbon steel, they discolour and even rust. The rust is easily washed away, and the discolouring is cosmetic only. Some people think that the discoloured blade looks dirty. These people tend to prefer stainless steel blades that always stay shiny. The fact that these blades get dull faster doesn't seem to concern users for whom the appearance of a blade is more important than its function.

The type of blade configuration and material that you decide to purchase is your personal decision. Please avoid peelers that claim to be multifunctional or those where the blade can be hidden by sliding it back into the handle. These fancier designs are hard to properly wash and tend to have poorly designed blades.

There is also the choice between serrated and plain cutting-edged blades. I have both types. Serrated peelers often remove less outer material from the carrot than plain peelers. Serrated peelers leave the carrot surface covered with fine grooves, which may or may not be an advantage depending on how the carrot is used in the final preparation. I find that serrated peelers slow me down when I have many pounds of carrots to pare. They are traditionally better for peeling the skins of overripe fruit but provide no advantage for hard vegetables.

No matter which style of peeler I use, my method for paring a carrot is the same. Carrots are always pared from their middle to their ends. Hold the carrot in your non-peeler hand by one of its ends in a manner that allows you to roll the carrot around its central axis. Support the other end on your cutting board. I slightly rest my holding hand on the board, too. With the blade held at a right angle to the carrot axis, draw the peeler from the middle to the end resting on your cutting board. After a strip of the 'skin' is removed, roll your carrot slightly towards you to expose a new area of the surface to be removed. The trick is to only roll the carrot enough so that you do not leave any unpared carrot between each pass with your peeler, but at the same time, you should not pare the same area twice. Once you pare one end, the carrot is flipped around, and you pare the other end in the same manner. With a little practice, this method allows for the high-speed paring required when faced with a large sack of needy carrots.

I leave the tip of the carrot with a little 'skin' since this part is often discarded during any further preparation. The crown or shoulder can either be trimmed away with a knife or pared with the peeler held in your hand in a manner like the choke grip for a paring knife that is discussed later. If the collar is shallow, the end of the carrot can be cleaned with the peeler at the same time you clean the crown. If the collar is deep, a large chef's knife is the best tool for you to quickly remove the whole crown.

Paring and trimming carrots is not a high-wire act. Always be sure to support the carrot on your board when paring, and against your thumb when trimming.

Knives for cutting carrots

As a teacher of knife skills, a historian who researches their history, and a speaker on culinary knives, I generally run into two types of knife-users. The first type buys inexpensive knives and then buys new ones when these get dull. The second type buys expensive knives and then proceeds to ruin them through improper use, poor cleaning, and lack of maintenance. It is rare that I find a kitchen where the knives are both sharp and treated properly. If you want to know where you fit in, view the video on my website (https://rd.hertzmann.com/?etvx). There you'll find everything you need to know about how to purchase, use, maintain and store your kitchen cutlery.

The best knives for working with carrots are long, thin chef's knives and short-bladed paring knives. Of these two, essentially all work can be accomplished with a chef's knife, which is sometimes called a cook's knife or French knife. The blade should be at least 23 cm (9 in) long. On the maximum side, 31 cm (12 ¼ in) is about as long as most people can handle. The spine of the blade, the edge opposite the cutting edge, should be narrow and rounded. A knife with a heavy spine may be appropriate to disjoint chickens, but for stiff, hard vegetables like carrots, heavy-spine knives are more likely to break off a piece of the carrot rather than smoothly cut it.

The chef's knife configuration makes it easy to slice against your cutting board since your holding-hand fingers have clearance between the handle and your board. Offset bread knives with serrated or wavy edges also provide finger clearance, but since the blade is ground on only one side, true vertical cutting is difficult. These knives generally pull to the left when you slice with them. They are probably okay for rough cutting, but any precise or consistent cut is difficult with this type of knife.

European-style *santoku* knives have finger clearance, but their blades are often too short and their cutting edges too straight for proper slicing. Sufficient blade length is needed for making lengthwise cuts on long pieces of carrot, especially if your knife skills are just beginning to develop. Traditional Chinese slicing cleavers and Japanese *santokus* and *nakiris* can also be used, but my experience with students is that these knives take substantially longer to master. Once again, their blades tend to be a bit short for normal slicing. The typical motion used by experienced cooks with either of these knife patterns is to simultaneously slice and move downwards in a forward motion. If you try this with a Japanese *usuba*, the slicing motion is further complicated by the single-bevel cutting edge that wants to pull towards your holding hand. However, if you wish to cut a carrot into a *katsuramuki* cut, you'll need an *usuba*. With most other knife patterns, you'll hit your knuckles against your board when you try to properly slice.

It is probably more important with carrots than other, softer vegetables to always slice rather chop or push with your knife. Chopping is a linguistic mistake leftover from when we used special chopping knives in the kitchen. None of the preparations in this book call for 'chopped' carrots. Likewise, all cutting should be by slicing. Rocking a knife by leaving the tip in place on your board is still a form of pushing or chopping and not safe. With rocking, the blade is still being moved perpendicular to the cut, which requires more force. Whether the tip of the board is in contact with your cutting board or not, the blade should always move forward and backward in a slicing motion.

Using knives

Most untrained chef's-knife users hold their kitchen knives the same as they learned to hold their dinner knife when they were a toddler. They extend their forefinger (pointer or index finger) down along the spine of the knife to add additional downward pressure. This 'granny' grip does not control a chef's knife as well as a pinch grip, the grip you see most professional chefs use. The pinch grip is very simple: Pinch the blade with your thumb and forefinger just in front of the handle. In this position, your fingers should be in contact with the end of the handle and the start of the blade. Finally, wrap your three remaining fingers firmly, but not too tight, over the handle.

The food being cut should be held with your free hand so that the first segment of your forefinger is flat against the side of the blade. As you slice, you should feel the side of the blade move lightly against your nail and the surface of the first knuckle of the finger (see the photo opposite page 29). If you keep your finger tip straight and pointing down with the side of the blade against it when you slice, you cannot cut yourself. Just be careful to not be distracted and let your finger angle backward – then you will cut yourself. The added benefit of this method is that your finger becomes a guide for the knife. It is faster to place your finger tip where you want to cut and then bring the side of the blade up next to it than it is to try to position the blade without a guide. You'll also find that with your finger leading the way, your results are more uniform, consistent, and fast.

If, as an alternative to using a peeler, you are using a paring knife to scrape a carrot, hold the knife in a pinch grip as you would with a larger chef's knife. On the rare occasion when you may be using the tip of a paring knife to perform some detail work on a carrot, hold the knife in a choke grip. With a choke grip, your forefinger and maybe your middle finger wrap around the blade with your remaining fingers around the handle. It's as if you are making a fist over the whole knife. The cutting edge is directed towards your thumb. When using a paring knife held in a choke grip, use your thumb to support the food item being cut. Don't let the knife slide in your hand, only on the food. I use the tip of a short paring knife held in choke grip to neatly trim the stalks and to scrape the collars and crowns of small carrots. The blade should be not be any longer than 9 cm (3½ in). The handle should also be short and lightweight.

When cutting carrots on your cutting board, always stand directly facing your board, and work in the centre of your board. Don't be forced into working into a corner of your board by crowding the surface with foodstuff. The direction of the slicing should be at an angle that is between being parallel to the front of your board and at forty-five degrees off parallel.

Use the cutting edge of the knife only for cutting. If you want to move the cut food out of the way – flip the knife over and use the spine or raise the cutting edge off the board a small amount. If you don't scrape along your board with your knife and slice rather than chop, you'll keep your knife feeling sharp much longer. You'll also find that a few proper swipes with the correct steel will renew the cutting edge for quite a while. Once again, the video on my website (https://rd.hertzmann.com/?etvx) describes all of this in detail.

Slicing carrots with a knife

For many of the various preparations in this book you'll either use the carrots whole, or maybe rough cut them into shorter pieces. On some occasions you'll need to divide the carrots into more precise pieces. In doing so, you'll be slicing the carrots one or more times. Simple slices only require a single cut, matchsticks or *bâtonnets* require two cuts, and cubes necessitate three.

Simple slices

You can change the characteristics of a carrot slice simply by changing the angle of your knife cut with respect to the central axis of the root. If your knife is at a right angle to the carrot's axis, you are cutting the carrot into what are called 'rounds' or 'coins'. The thickness of the slices can easily be made consistent by always moving your holding finger the same distance and always holding the blade absolutely vertical as you make each slice. As your knife angle rotates towards your carrot-holding hand, the slices become more oval-shaped. When the blade axis is almost parallel to the carrot axis, you are simply splitting the carrot into long pieces. When cutting the carrot into ovals, if you cut pieces of even thickness, each oval is a little shorter than the previous one because the carrot is tapered. If you want ovals to be the same length, you need to adjust your knife angle on each cut to be slightly more towards being parallel to the carrot axis.

To slice the carrot, lay it on your cutting board parallel to the front with the narrow end toward your non-knife hand. Place your knife so it is pointing about thirty degrees from the front of your board. Hold the

plan the length of the slice by
holding the knife over the carrot

move the knife to the end
to make the first slice

blade is always vertical, touching the
forefinger at the knuckle and nail

the forefinger position
determines the thickness of the slice

carrot firmly, with your fingertip pressing straight down on the top of the carrot. Position a chef's knife held with a pinch grip so the flat of the blade rests against the flat side of the tip of your forefinger. This way, your forefinger serves as a guide for the knife. Start each slice with the cutting edge of the blade parallel to your cutting board. As you move the knife forward and then backward, a slice is made. Try to exert a minimal amount of downward pressure and let your knife do the work. After each cut move your forefinger a distance equal to the desired thickness of the next slice. It is important that the flat of the blade always remains in contact with the flat surface of your forefinger. If the carrot is difficult to cut and requires many back-and-forth moves along with applying pressure on it, your knife may be dull and need to be sharpened.

Matchsticks, julienne, or bâtonnets

Cutting carrots into strips, whether called matchsticks, *julienne*, or *bâtonnets*, is the second step after first cutting a carrot into long, oval-shaped slices. Stack three or four carrot slices at a time on your cutting board. If your slices are quite thick, it may be easier to work with just one or two slices at a time since the slices tend to slide when stacked. Slice as instructed above with the blade resting against the flat side of the tip of your non-knife forefinger. After each cut, move your forefinger a distance equal to the desired width of the next cut. Ideally, the width of this cut should be the same as the thickness of the slice, so the resulting strips have a perfectly square cross section. Remember to slice and not to provide much downward force.

The above method is not the traditional process for cutting a carrot into strips. In the traditional method, the carrot is first cut into sections whose length matches the desired length of the final strips. Each section is then squared off by slicing off the rounded sides of the section in lengthwise cuts. Once a square 'log' of carrot is produced, the log is cut lengthwise into strips of the desired size. The traditional method produces a sizable amount of waste. In the past, when restaurant kitchens produced stocks on a daily basis, all clean vegetable scraps went into the stockpot. Today, they tend to end up in the trash.

plan for a 1.5 cm (½ in) space between the tip and the cut

roll carrot towards the front of the board and make another slice at the same angle and spacing

blade is always vertical, touching the forefinger at the knuckle and nail

although random in appearance, roll cut pieces all cook at the same rate

A major difference between the traditional method of producing strips and the method I described at the beginning of this section is that the traditional method produces strips with a squared-off end, and the newer method produces strips with an angled end. The angled ends can be attractive in the finished dish, especially if this method is being used to cut a vegetable where the skins are a different colour than the flesh, such as courgettes. (Remember, the carrot is just a stand-in in this book for many other vegetables.) If the strips are being cut as a preliminary step to producing cubes, then the squared-off strips may be a better method to use. If the cubes are to be large or quite noticeable, use the traditional method. Overall, I tend to use the newer method because it produces results faster while producing little waste.

Dicing

The process to produce cubes of carrots, commonly called a dice, is simply an extension of the previous steps. Gather your previously cut strips into a stack, with all the strips parallel to one another. With the fingertips of your non-knife hand in a vertical position, hold the stack firmly in place. Sometimes, it helps to use your thumb and little finger to support the pile from the sides. Slice as previously instructed. In many cases, you actually have to lift and drop your fingers ever so slightly so the stack of strips stays intact. Ideally, the width of this cut is equal to the thickness of the strips, so the resulting dice are perfect cubes.

Roll cut

For braising, stewing, and roasting, carrots can be cut into irregular shapes of approximately the 'same' size using the roll-cut technique. Hold a peeled carrot firmly on your cutting board, parallel to the front, with your non-knife hand. Hold a chef's knife with a pinch grip at about a thirty-degree angle to the carrot and near the carrot's tip. Make your first slice close to the tip. Roll the carrot ninety degrees towards the front of the board but maintain the same distance to the front. Position your knife about 1.5 cm (½ in) towards your non-knife hand and slice.

After each cut, position the knife the same distance and direction. The 'length' of each cut should be constant, even as the portion of carrot being cut becomes wider.

Grating carrots

The number of vegetable graters on the market is mindnumbing. There are multiple variations from traditional flat or box-shaped, nickel-plated steel graters, to hand-crank graters, to standalone electric graters, to attachments for stand mixers and food processors. Older graters are made by punching and stamping the metal; new graters are made by etching the holes and sharpening the edges. Some modern graters even recommend that you wear a cut-resistant glove when you use them. You probably have several graters already tucked away in various places in your kitchen.

Most graters are designed to cut a carrot into short, crude strips, and for the activity for which they are designed, they work just fine. Hand graters are sufficient for grating one or two carrots, but for grating a bushel's worth, a powered grater is preferred.

Mandolins

A subset of graters is the mandolin. These are used to cut carrots into long, flat, thin slices or into even, fine strips. Mandolins can produce very consistent results. There are two major design differences in mandolins. Traditional French-style mandolins position the blade so the sharp edge is at a right angle to the direction the food is moving. Japanese-style mandolins, which are now also made under European- and American-company names, position the cutting edge at an acute angle. Given a blade of equal sharpness, the Japanese-style mandolin requires much less force to cut.

With either type of mandolin, always use the safety guard provided in the original packaging. You did save the guard when you threw the box away, didn't you?

I use these tools differently to the way shown on the package pictures. I hold the mandolin so the bed the carrot travels on is straight up-and-down, and I view down the bed so I can always see where my fingertips are in relation to the blade. I support the bottom end of the mandolin on a towel so it doesn't slip.

You can easily cut yourself very badly on a mandolin if you are not mindful of what you are doing. Every professional can tell you stories of accidents that happened to them or to others. I developed my safer way of using a mandolin after removing a fingertip at the start of a four-hour prep session for a thirty-person party. With a little duct tape, I persevered, but it wasn't fun. When you treat your mandolin with boatloads of respect, it becomes less scary.

Juicing carrots

There seems to be four types of powered juicers on the market today. I say 'seems' because the manufacturers often describe their 'unique' juicing process with proprietary terms to differentiate their product from the competition, and not all juicers are available in all areas. The common types of juicers can be divided into juice extractors, also known as centrifugal juicers, and masticating, auger, or cold press juicers. The later works by slowly crushing and mashing its victims. Juice extractors use a rapidly spinning disk to grate the unsuspecting vegetable into tiny pieces that are then spun to separate the juice from the pulp. Auger extractors are available with either a single augur or duals augurs. Less well known are two stage juicers, the original type, that first grinds the material, which is packed in a porous bag, and then the machine presses the bags to extract the juice.

For scientific purposes – which should work just as well at home – carrots are juiced by combining cut-up pieces with an amount of water equal to one-fifth of the weight of the carrots in a liquidiser. The carrots are then puréed and sieved to produce the juice. As to which method of juicing is superior, I have no opinion.

Fifteen years ago, I found an inexpensive centrifugal juicer on sale at a local department store for less than £20. That's what I still use. It's a pain in the rear to clean, and there are some tiny crevices in its housing that are now permanently dirty. It seems to work okay, but I doubt it's as efficient as a newer unit for ten times the price.

Liquidising carrots

Liquidisers and food processors are often confused by the average person. They appear to have the same function, but they don't. Liquidisers are designed to purée food with a blade that shears the contents of its jar. The blade acts more like a scissor than a knife and has the potential for producing a much smaller particle than is possible with a food processor. To purée large pieces, some liquid is required so that the pieces don't just create a dry pile above the blade. Expensive, high horsepower units do a much better job of puréeing than the inexpensive, underpowered units. High-horsepower units move the tip of the blade at a higher speed and have enough power so that the speed is maintained, even in a resistive food environment. It is a combination of the high tip speed and the tip configuration that produces a smaller particle size and a smoother purée. If you read a recipe that calls for straining the liquidiser-jar contents after puréeing it, then the recipe author was using an underpowered liquidiser. I've never had to strain even the stringiest of vegetables after puréeing in a high-powered model.

Some foods need to be liquidised for several minutes. During this time, the food being puréed gets warmer – a result of the friction produced by the high-speed blade. If you're making a puréed soup, the liquidiser can heat it at the same time as it produces the purée. But be careful, puréeing a fruit or vegetable high in pectin can produce a solid gel if the mixture become hot enough to cause the pectin molecules to crosslink.

Immersion liquidisers

A subset of the standard jar-style liquidisers is the immersion, stick, or handheld liquidiser. These are designed to purée food directly in the pot or bowl it is already in. Most commonly available versions are inexpensive and not very effective. There is one exception. The Bamix immersion liquidiser is by comparison quite expensive, but it achieves a much higher tip speed, and it comes with multiple, interchangeable blades that cut, whisk, foam, and beat. The other immersion liquidisers work okay for some uses, but this one does everything it does better.

Processing carrots

Whereas liquidisers have blades that shear the food, processors have blades that cut or slice. Some food processors come with a collection of bowls of different sizes. In my experience, only the largest bowls paired with the larger blades are effective. The maximum number of revolutions per minute is the same for large and small bowls. Since the tip speed of the blade is a function of the blade's radius and the speed at which it is revolving, larger blades produce faster tip speeds which in turn produces better results. Yes, mini-food processors may be easier to store and clean, but the truth is that they just don't work all that well for all jobs.

For processing jobs where the sides of the bowl need to be scraped down multiple times, I use the lid as the on-off switch. This saves taking time for the extra step of manipulating the on-off switch.

One aspect of food processing that I learned on one of my early *stages* was to process for many minutes to either get a better purée, or at times, radically change the characteristics of the purée. Don't be afraid of processing for many minutes past when it looks like the food seems to be fully puréed. (Unless your processor is underpowered, in which case you may burn out the motor.) You may be surprised to find that the heat produced by the process causes interesting changes in taste, texture, and appearance.

General equipment for cooking carrots

For the most part, the equipment for cooking carrots is that found in any modern kitchen. In some cases, the tools and equipment you have may hinder you without you knowing it. Often, the older designs for tools were better than newer designs. Many so-called improvements have been made to induce customers to purchase a newer version of something that they already had. For example, many of the modern whisk designs do not work as well as the wooden-handled whisks of fifty years ago. The original, handle-less, Microplane-brand grater worked great. The newer version with handles in twelve colours is not an improvement, and aspects of the newer designs make working with the grater more difficult.

For the most part, I use industrial kitchen equipment rather than that I find at the national chain cookware store in the mall down the street. I use industrial, stainless-steel mixing bowls that stack well and come in a multitude of sizes. I only have three of the same-size giant bowls I use for mixing dough, but in the smaller sizes I have at least six of each size. All twenty-four mixing bowls stack into a single space on my shelf. These are wide, shallow bowls. I have an additional twelve that are deep with flat bottoms that sit on the shelf between the other bowls and the five different sizes of glass prep bowls I have in quantities of at least six. I am never hindered by a lack of bowls when I prep and cook.

In a similar vein, I have a multitude of industrial, stainless-steel spoons, tongs, ladles, and turners. There is also a collection of different-sized rubber spatulas in half-dozen quantities. These are not the fancy spatulas in multiple colours and patterns that I see in most houses, but cheap white ones that get thrown away when damaged.

Stamped, stainless-steel spoons that come in various sizes, both with and without holes, may not look as pleasant as the expensive ones at your local department store, but they do the job. For the price of a single, heavy-handled, German spoon I can buy a dozen of the industrial spoons. With most hand tools in the kitchen, the industrial versions may be less attractive, but they'll be cheaper and work better than the fashion-forward items designed to attract home cooks.

Two ancient kitchen tools that are often forgotten about are pieces of cloth and heavy string. Years ago, I purchased an expensive square of butter muslin from a cheesemaking-supply company. The cloth was helpful for many tasks, but I kept washing it out because it was too expensive to discard after one use. Then one day I walked into an old-time fabric store and bought a yard of bleached, 100% cotton muslin of the loosest thread count that the store had. This muslin was soft and not stiff. It worked great for every straining use I threw at it. I've now been back to the store several times to restock. Purchasing a single yard from the bolt yields a piece that is one by three yards. That's a lot of cloth for my kitchen, and the cost is under £2. Now when done with a piece of the cloth, I just toss it out. I figure that I don't spend more than a few pennies for each piece that I use.

Often, I need some way to fasten together the bags I make from the muslin. For that task I keep a cone of heavy, cotton string. I can fashion a bag for solid spices out of a small piece of the cloth and tie it together with the string. One end of the string is kept long to ease fishing the bag from the pot of whatever it is in. The string is also handy for other uses that crop up from time to time, such a tying a bundle of herbs into a *bouquet garnie* or tying a roast. When saturated with grease or oil, the cotton string can even withstand a pretty hot oven without charring.

Contrary to how all of the above may sound, I don't have a large kitchen. Except for my work top, none of my built-in appliances are full size. Two people can work at once only if we coordinate our dance. Since moving from a much larger space, I have adapted to more stacking and having to unpack a shelf to get to an item at the back. If my meal preparation is for more than half a dozen people, I must beg for refrigerator space from my neighbours.

The size of your kitchen should not limit your cooking. Bigger is not always better.

Raw Methods

1 - 9

1. Raw Carrots

No one knows when cooks and philosophers began debating what actions were required for a dish to be referred to as cooked. For many, heat must be applied to the raw foods for them to be cooked. For now, let's assume that the process of cooking includes raw carrots that no longer look like those you purchased earlier at the market, and the handling and subsequent minor processing of a raw carrot constitutes a cooking method for this collection.

During my youth in California in the 1950s, many restaurants placed a dish of raw vegetables on your table when the server came to take your order. Typically, the dish contains pitted black olives, celery sticks, green onions – also called scallions, spring onions, Welsh onions, bunching onions, salad onions, and more, depending on your location – and carrot sticks. Except for the olives, which needed to be cured before they could be eaten, the other vegetables were simply washed and trimmed for service. In the end, these vegetables could be dull.

The French make their raw vegetables *(crudités)* more interesting by serving them with one or more dipping sauces. Sometimes the sauce is plain mayonnaise, and sometimes the mayonnaise is flavoured. Whether your interest is in the French or American style, both are more complicated than they need to be.

Starting with good-sized pared carrots, the fattest you can find, use a swivel-peeler to slice long flat strips of carrot. The peeler limits the thickness to quite thin. Trim the strips into bite-sized pieces, maybe about 5 cm (2 in) long. Soak the strips for an hour or so in ice water to give them a little curl and a bit of stiffness.

Before serving, drain the carrot strips quite well on kitchen paper or even a tea towel. The carrot may stain the towel, but the stains should wash out easily. Because of the cold water, the carrot strip should have curled a bit.

The simplest way of serving the carrot strips is to season them with one or more dried, ground spices. Use your imagination. Raid your spice collection and check out the possibilities. Cinnamon and ginger are two readily available ground spices that work well with raw carrot. Usually, all that is required is a fine pinch or two. Spice blends like curry powder, garum marsala, and dehydrated chicken stock all work well. Blends that contain dried herbs may require a little contact time with the raw carrot to rehydrate the herb leaves if they are not ground very fine. Basil, thyme, and oregano leaves, when rehydrated, are a fine combination.

Any variety of modern salad dressing is also worth a try. A bowl of carrot strips can be served alongside a host of dressings as an homage to a traditional French *crudité* presentation. Standard thick dips such as hummus, guacamole, or flavoured sour cream work, but thin dips like salsa probably do not.

Working with raw carrot strips, you can decide whether the flavour of the raw carrot predominates, by using an accompaniment that accents the flavour of the carrot, or whether the flavour of the accompaniment predominates and the carrot is just a convenient means of transporting it to your mouth.

2. Carrot Juice

Although juice may be defined as 'the liquid obtained from or present in fruit or vegetables', we tend to differentiate between fruits and vegetables where juice is obvious when the item is cut, such as tomatoes and oranges, and hard items, such as apples and carrots, which require more aggressive methods to obtain their juice. Juice can be extracted from oranges and tomatoes by hand squeezing. For carrots and apples, more forceful mechanization is required.

Since the introduction in the 1930s of the first juicing machines, these machines have been popular with consumers for producing drinks high in nutrients. In the case of carrots, the juice is high in beta-carotene, a form of Vitamin A. Although initially popular, issues develop for many owners. Juicers are large. Some are difficult to clean. Most make a lot of noise. The fruits and vegetables needed to serve the beast can be expensive. I wonder how many machines remain a delight to their owners after their initial flurry of use, and how many become a dust collector or a jumble-sale item?

Besides producing carrot juice, juicing machines produce carrot pulp, which is normally considered a waste product, but don't toss the pulp in the trash bin. The pulp is finely grated carrot with about half the water content found in the original carrot. Many of the following methods, such as 12. Carrot Dip (page 75), include uses for the pulp.

My interest in carrot juice is a matter of flavour and texture rather than nutrients. Those are just an added benefit. Carrot juice is mostly made up of suspended solids. The percentage of water, carbohydrates, and sugars are about the same in solid carrots as in their juice. The amount of fibre, which is mostly cellulose, is reduced by about three-quarters.

Pasteurized Juice

Once produced, carrot juice stays fresh only for a day or two, even when refrigerated. Pasteurization helps stabilize the juice and make it safer, but the taste may lack some of the flavour components found in raw juice. For most home uses, a vigorous washing of the carrots is enough to clean them, although anyone with immune system issues should maybe avoid raw juice.

To pasteurize the juice, its temperature must be raised to 70 °C (160 °F). Once the entire volume of juice reaches the desired temperature, the juice can be rapidly cooled in a water-ice bath.

If you have an immersion circulator that be disassembled and easily cleaned, the juice can quickly be pasteurized. Just set the circulator to the pasteurization temperature and when the juice comes to temperature, cool it as mentioned previously. The circulator prevents exposing the juice to higher than necessary heat.

Filtered juice

The juice can be drunk as it comes from your juicer with all its particles of a variety of sizes. The larger pieces can usually be seen floating to the surface and gathering around the edges of the juice container. They are less likely to stay in suspension as are the smaller particles. Filtered juice looks nicer than the unfiltered juice when combined with other ingredients. I like to filter the juice through a standard paper coffee filter to remove the larger particles.

Be patient so the maximum amount of juice passes through the filter. Don't discard the particles caught in the coffee filter. The mush left in the filter is useful as a raw carrot paste (see 7. Carrot Dressing, page 54).

Clarified Juice

For a more surprising carrot juice, clarify it. Clarified carrot juice is as clear as water, but it has a slight, brownish tint. The process involves mixing the carrot juice with a material that agglomerates any loose particles present in it. Once the particles are sequestered, the remaining liquid can be drained off. For the agglomeration we use agar, an unbranched polysaccharide obtained from various kinds of red seaweed used as a thickener in foods. When added to liquids in the proper proportions, polysaccharides cross-link to form a structure that inhibits the movement of water molecules. The whole mass forms into a gel. Gels are susceptible to syneresis, a process where water droplets weep from the gel structure. We'll take advantage of this process to separate the clarified juice from the carrot solids which remain captured by the gel.

Agar is available as a powder – its modern form – and in sheets called *kanten* in Japanese – its traditional form. It is easier to precisely measure powdered agar, but some people believe *kanten* to be more natural. Both are used at a ratio of 0.2% to gel juice for clarification.

Start by measuring the weight of juice you wish to clarify. The juice can be raw as it comes from the juicer, or filtered. Multiply the juice weight by 0.002 to determine the amount of agar to use. For example, if you have a bowl with 850 grams of juice, you'll need just 1.7 grams of agar (850 times 0.002 equals 1.7).

Place a third of the juice in a saucepan over high heat. While vigorously stirring with a whisk, slowly sprinkle the agar over the surface of the liquid. Keep stirring until none of the agar is visible. As vapour starts coming off the surface of the liquid, lower the heat. Continue whisking for about three more minutes until the liquid slightly thickens. There's no need to boil the liquid since the agar melts at about 85 °C (185 °F), but the agar needs to be fully hydrated.

Combine the hot carrot juice with the cold carrot juice in the original bowl. Stir enough to evenly combine the two. Place the bowl in your refrigerator until the solution is gloopy. It does not have to be fully set. In my fridge, the process takes about thirty minutes, but it may take a longer or shorter time in yours.

While the juice-agar solution is thickening, set up a coffee filter in a funnel over a collection jar. I use the funnel of an old drip coffee set-up over a glass jar. Mine is designed for #4 filters.

When the juice-agar combination is quite gloopy, gently transfer it to the filter-lined funnel. Depending upon the degree of gelling, the agar may release all the liquid in half an hour, or the process may take overnight. Be patient. Don't stir the combination. If the chunks appear too large, they can be broken up gently with a dinner knife. Even though the filter is present, the secret to a very clear juice is to disturb the filter contents as little as possible.

The clear juice can be drunk as is or used as an ingredient for a slew of cocktails (see 3. Cocktails, page 47), soda (see 4. Soda, page 49), or syrup (see 46. Carrot Syrup, page 174).

3. Carrot Cocktails

Screwdriver

There are classic cocktails based on tomato juice, orange juice, and lime juice. Why not carrot juice? As far as I can tell, none of the cocktails in the official list from the International Bartenders Association (IBA) use carrot juice, but that won't stop us. Let's start by enhancing the vodka in a Screwdriver with filtered carrot juice:

50 ml (1½ fl oz) vodka
100 ml (3 oz) filtered carrot juice
15 ml (½ oz) lemon juice

Pour the vodka and carrot juice into an ice-filled rocks glass. Stir well.

Gimlet

The Gimlet is nowhere to be found on the IBA list of cocktails, but I know it's a classic because it's what my mother drank:

50 ml (1½ fl oz) dry gin
100 ml (3 fl oz) clarified carrot juice
15 ml (½ fl oz) lemon juice

Add the ingredients to a cocktail shaker. Top with ice. Shake to chill. Strain into a chilled coupe.

Bloody Mary

The Bloody Mary is a common starter drink for young drinkers – maybe because of the garnish or the fact they can't taste the alcohol. So that the carrot juice has a thicker consistency, similar to tomato juice, start with raw carrot juice and thicken it with 0.1% xanthan gum by weight (multiply juice weight by .001). The gum needs to be sheered into the juice, not simply mixed. To do so, place the juice in a beaker, and stir rapidly with an immersion liquidiser. Slowly sprinkle the xanthan gum over the juice. Continue liquidising until the mixture thickens evenly. The thickened juice lasts quite a while in your refrigerator.

50 ml (1½ fl oz) vodka
100 ml (3 fl oz) thickened carrot juice
15 ml (½ fl oz) lemon juice
2 to 3 dashes Valentina or Choluloa hot sauce
2 to 3 dashes Worcestershire sauce
fine salt
freshly ground black pepper

Add all the ingredients to an ice-filled highball glass. Stir well. Garnish with a carrot curl. (See 1. Raw Carrots, page 41)

It's easy to create new cocktails by substituting carrot juice for an existing non-alcoholic ingredient. You should also try creating new carrot juice cocktails from scratch with whatever is in your house.

4. Carrot Soda

Commercial sodas are made by dissolving carbon dioxide gas into a mixture of flavoured syrup and water. When bottled under pressure, the gas is forced to stay dissolved in the liquid by the pressurized space between the cap and the liquid.

The process can be easily duplicated in a home kitchen using a siphon jar. (Be sure to familiarize yourself with the jar's directions.) Siphon jars are metal jars designed to be pressurized with gas, usually carbon dioxide or nitrous oxide. They are available in half- and one-litre sizes. The gas comes in small metal cartridges. The siphon jar is usually marked to indicate the maximum fill level. Don't overfill the jar.

Either plain carrot juice or diluted carrot-juice syrup can be carbonated. If using plain carrot juice, I suggest that it should be filtered to eliminate larger particles that may clog the dispensing mechanism on the siphon. Carrot juice syrup can be diluted by up to half with filtered water. (I recommend using syrup made by adding sugar rather than clarified juice syrup since less juice is required to produce the finished product. See 46. Carrot Syrup, page 174.) In either case, the liquid is placed in the siphon jar, and valve head tightly attached. Half-litre jars should be charged with one carbon dioxide gas cartridge. (Nitrous oxide gas is used for whipped cream and similar foams.) One-litre jars should be charged with two cartridges. Shake the jar until it sounds like the gas is incorporated. If not dispensing immediately, refrigerate the jar with its contents.

Before dispensing the soda, give the siphon another shake. Set the siphon in your sink, nozzle pointed up. Place a small glass over the tip of the nozzle, and fully discharge the gas into the glass. If the siphon is not too full, only gas should come out. Once the pressure is fully discharged, unscrew the valve head and set it aside. Pour your soda directly from the siphon jar into serving glasses.

If you don't have a siphon, a pretty good alternative can be achieved using syrup and any form of sparkling water. I use equal amounts of syrup and carbonated water poured into a tall glass with a little ice. Stir well with a long spoon, and you have a ready-to-drink soda.

5. Carrot Gazpacho

Producing a pleasant, warm carrot soup, or even a cooked carrot soup served at room temperature or chilled, is easy because cooking increases the natural sweetness and moderates the sometime obnoxious crispness of the soup. Producing a cold carrot soup that has never been heated is problematic: Carrots are very crispy, even in very small pieces. Most people don't relish a crunchy, cold soup. On the opposite end of the crunchy perspective, carrot juice could be served as soup, but that is just juice served in a bowl instead of a glass.

A traditional interpretation

The typical never-cooked cold soup is gazpacho. The base for most gazpachos is tomatoes, fruit that when ripe and cut up is never described as crunchy. Some gazpachos are puréed with bread to make a thickened, cold food. Why not add bread, or even bread crumbs, to raw carrot juice? This is referred to as making a panade, a traditional French manner of thickening liquids. Using a soft sandwich bread produces a smoother soup. Using a crusty style of bread produces a soup with a coarser texture. A bread with a strong flavour also flavours the soup, a bland bread adds less flavour. After the bread is well-soaked in raw juice, unlike the traditional manner of pounding ingredients in a mortar, we'll use a liquidiser. How long to blend for is up to you. The longer you blend, the smoother the result – within the limits of your liquidiser – I often blend for a full five minutes. Likewise, the amount of bread used affects how thick the soup is.

Before emptying the liquidiser jar, taste your soup. At a minimum, it probably needs a bit of salt to bring out the full flavour of the carrots. Other flavour directions you can travel to is to add ground cumin and a touch of acid, such as of lime juice or wine vinegar. The strength and type are up to you. After each addition, blitz briefly in the liquidiser and taste the result. Always taste as you go. Another direction you can go is to add some chili sauce, the choice of type and hotness is yours. If you want to be adventurous, add some unsweetened cocoa powder to the blend!

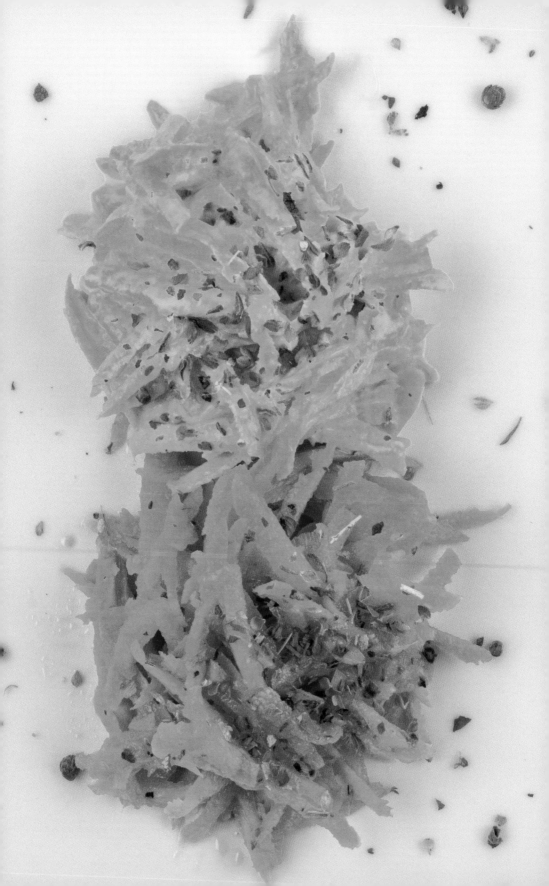

A modern interpretation

For a more modern, totally smooth cold soup, shear a little xanthan gum into raw juice. Work within a range of 1 to 3 g (0.03 to 0.1 oz) of gum for each litre of raw juice. For the shearing, I use either an immersion or a stand liquidiser. Find the proper consistency for your taste. Remember that too much xanthan gum can lead to a mucous-like texture. Season the carrot soup in a manner as mentioned above.

6. Carrot Slaw

The carrot salad sold at my local deli consists of shredded carrots, sultanas, mayonnaise, sugar, salt, and pepper. It's not bad. It's typical of the carrot salads I've eaten in the southern regions of America. I once had a phenomenal carrot and garlic salad at a Uyghur restaurant in Brighton Beach, New York, that I have never been able to recreate. There are also the Japanese carrot salads I've had over the years where the carrots were slightly blanched to soften the crunch and remove the raw taste. Carrot salad can be great.

For this version of carrot salad, which qualifies as a slaw because the carrots are shredded, I decided to only minimally modify the main ingredient. Minimal if you don't consider shredding the carrot a major modification.

Make the salad

Clean a few carrots. Trim off the shoulders and any bad areas. Grate the carrots by hand or with the fine grating attachment of a food processor or other mechanical grater. The medium shredding blade on a Japanese mandolin is also satisfactory.

Gather the grated pieces in a bowl. Add some olive oil just until the wet appearance of the carrots shifts from watery to oily. You don't want a puddle in the bottom of your bowl. Add a splash of acid, either a vinegar or a citrus juice, to the salad to brighten the flavour. Or if you prefer, substitute a dollop of mayonnaise for the oil and acid. It can even be vegan mayonnaise. Mix in some salt and give the mixture a taste.

You can give the salad a bit more flavour by raiding your cupboard. Select a flavouring to add as an accent to the slaw. For me, I selected a Jordanian za'atar, but I also considered dried fenugreek leaves and Mexican oregano. Be creative! It's your slaw. You could even sneak a few sultanas in!

Once the flavouring is added, be sure to set the slaw aside to hydrate any dried herbs before serving.

7. Carrot Dressing

Most salad dressings are based on some form of an emulsion. Emulsions consist of fat and water divided into a dispersed phase and a continuous phase. Fine droplets of the dispersed phase are kept separate by the molecules of the continuous phase. Mayonnaise is a common example of an emulsion. In it, very tiny droplets of oil are kept separate by a small amount of water molecules. In most emulsions, the process is aided by a special ingredient called a surfactant. The surfactant coats each oil droplet with a layer of molecules aligned to aid in the constancy of the separation. In mayonnaise, the surfactant is usually the lecithin present in the egg yolk. The egg also supplies the water to the emulsion.

Mayonnaise is called a fat-in-water emulsion. Butter is another example. Homogenized milk is the opposite, a water-in-fat emulsion.

Emulsions such as mayonnaise are referred to as stable emulsions whereas a typical oil and vinegar salad dressing is considered an unstable emulsion since without a stabilizer, the dressing quickly separates. The stabilizer is often a gum such as gar gum or xanthan gum or a combination of the two.

Make the dressing

It's not easy to simply combine carrot juice with oil to form an emulsion, but a concentrated form of carrot can be combined with mayonnaise to make a dressing. When raw carrot juice is filtered in a coffee filter, as demonstrated in 2. Carrot Juice (page 42) the solid material that is filtered out can be harvested from the filter paper. Mixing this carrot 'paste' with mayonnaise produces the start of a salad dressing. A ratio of equal parts of mayonnaise and carrot paste is a good place to start. Taste the mixture after each addition and see if you like the way it's headed. The flavours mellow slightly when combined with a salad or other items. With this base, you can add a little acid, such as vinegar or lemon juice, salt and pepper, and my favourite, hot chili sauce. Ground cumin goes well with carrot. As does ground cinnamon. This dressing can also be used as a sauce for fried fish or a dip for french fries. It's quite versatile.

Make another dressing

Another way to make a carrot dressing is to start with a heavy foam. A foam is like an emulsion except the dispersed phase is gas and the continuous phase is a liquid. A foam is not a true emulsion. If we start by thickening raw carrot juice into a thick foam with xanthan gum, as we did in 3. Carrot Cocktails, page 47, we can use this as a base for many salad dressings. The simplest additions are vinegar or lemon juice, just a little, plus some salt and pepper. Modify the combination so that it tastes good to you. If the dressing becomes too thin, you can try shearing in some more xanthan gum.

8. Carrot Gelatine

The buffet-table gelatine dishes of my childhood consisted of aspics and gelatine moulds. Aspics were made from vegetable juices, most often tomato juice, and gelatine moulds were made from flavoured gelatine with pieces of fruit. The fanciest ones had layers of different coloured gelatine. Aspics were often augmented with a green mayonnaise dressing. I had a chance in 2010 to taste a tomato aspic with an avocado-mayonnaise. It was quite good. So, why not try a carrot aspic.

Is carrot aspic suspect?

You'll need a mould to make the aspic in. It can be a plain, round bowl or a fancy mould. There are even modern, silicone-rubber moulds that

grandma could only dream about. Before starting, measure the capacity of the mould. This determines how much juice you'll need. Although you could use agar as the gelling agent, gelatine produces a more favourable result. Gelatine melts close to mouth temperature, so the mouthfeel of the finished dish is more pleasant. Agar can be heated so you could experiment with a warm aspic.

Gelatine comes in two principle forms: sheets and powder. If you're going to use sheets, purchase 'silver' gelatine, or a type with a bloom strength of 160. If you purchase 'gold' gelatine, or a type with a bloom strength of 225, you'll need to use less, 84% of the amount specified below. You'll need about 17 g (½ oz) of 'silver' sheet gelatine to gel 1 litre (4¼ cups) of juice. Sheet gelatine is soaked for a few seconds in water before adding to the liquid. See 11. Carrot Foam (page 71) for more information on converting gelatine quantities for different bloom-strength gelatines.

Most powdered gelatines provide a prescription on the pack as to how much liquid is gelled by how much gelatine. My package instructs me to use 14 g (5 tsp) of gelatine for 1 litre (4¼ cups) of liquid. According to other sources, my brand of powdered gelatine has a bloom strength of 225. Powder gelatine must be first bloomed in the cold liquid before heating.

Place about a fourth of your liquid – raw or filtered carrot juice, slightly salted – in a saucepan. If using powdered gelatine, bloom it in the juice before heating. The powder should float to the top. When it has swelled as much as it looks like it will, heat the juice until the gelatine melts. Stir the juice continuously. This should happen fast. If using sheet gelatine, the juice can be warmed before adding, but not hotter than you can put a finger into. Squeeze as much water as possible from the gelatine and add to the warm juice. All that should be required is a little stirring unless your juice is too cool.

When the gelatine has melted in the warm juice, add the combination to the rest of the juice, and stir. Pour the combination into the mould or dish. Set in your refrigerator to become solid. Overnight is usually good.

Unmould the aspic onto a plate for serving. If it doesn't want to release easily from the mould, soak the mould briefly in warm, not hot, water. To unmould, place the serving plate, upside down, over the mould and turn over quickly. The carrot salad dressing made with the xanthan gel is a good accompaniment (see 7. Carrot Dressing, page 54). Even plain whipped mayonnaise is good. Whipped mayonnaise is made by whisking mayonnaise until it is loose.

Would the Japanese like carrot *tokoroten*?

There's a Japanese dish called *tokoroten* that looks like clear pasta. It is commonly made with fish stock and agar. You need a *tokoroten* press for this dish although a close facsimile can be made with a slicing knife. This is fun to do with carrot juice.

The block of flavoured gelatine required for *tokoroten* is best made in a mould with square corners, but it's not a deal breaker. I use a Japanese cake pan with a removable bottom and square corners, but a small loaf pan would work almost as well. The raw carrot juice should be weighed and a third placed in a saucepan. Add 0.75% (total juice weight times 0.0075) powdered agar to the saucepan, turn up the heat, and whisk until the agar is fully hydrated, about three minutes. You'll know when it's ready when no more agar particles are visible, and the viscosity has thickened slightly. Stir the hot juice into the cold juice and pour the combination into the mould. Refrigerate until solid.

Agar gels are usually strong so a little shaking and gentle pulling should release the gelled juice from the mould. If you're using a knife to shape the *tokoroten* 'noodles', slice the block into long, square noodles of about 3 mm (⅛ in) on each side. The knife should be thin. A cheese wire also works. If using a *tokoroten* press, trim the block to fit the press, and push it through the grating at the end to cut the noodles.

The *tokoroten* can be eaten as is, sprinkled with a little salt, or dripped with a little rice vinegar and soy sauce.

9. Carrot Pickles

Before cooks possessed the ability to preserve food with refrigeration and freezing, techniques like drying, pickling, and smoking were commonly used to preserve meat, fish, and vegetables. Root vegetables were an exception.

Most root vegetables could be harvested in the summer and then stored in man-made caves until the spring. Carrots were often stored in barrels of dry sawdust with some of the sawdust separating one carrot from the next. Once in the barrel, the whole container went into the root cellar to keep cool. Even though carrots traditionally haven't been pickled for preservation, you can still pickle carrots just because the result tastes good.

There are two basic methods of pickling. The oldest form is probably bacterial fermentation brought about by immersing the vegetable into a salt-based brine. Almost as old is acid fermentation, usually done by immersing the vegetable in wine or vinegar.

Bacterial and plain salt fermentations

The *lactobacillus* bacteria responsible for bacterial fermentation is anaerobic. This means that it works when there is no air present. This environment is usually created by keeping the item being fermented covered with brine. There are many products available that adapt a canning jar to make it an anaerobic pickling container.

To ferment carrots, start by choosing a jar to pickle the carrots in. A clean, wide-mouth canning jar with straight sides makes it easy to get the carrots in and out. I find that a 500 ml (2 cup) size to be about right. Pare enough carrots to fill the jar when cut to length. If you can find small, skinny carrots, don't bother to pare them. Only cut them to a length where they fit in the jar while leaving about 1 to 2 cm (⅜ to ¾ in) headspace. After paring, if the carrots are thicker than about 1 cm (⅜ in), split them lengthwise into two or more pieces with a chef's knife.

Once the carrots all fit in the canning jar, remove them and determine how much they weigh. Add 3% salt by multiplying the weight by 0.03 and measuring out that much salt, or just do it by eye. Table salt is fine, but not the iodized type. Avoid fancy, unrefined salt for pickling because it may contain some calcium. The calcium can cause the pectin in the carrot to crosslink and become tough. I prefer the finer grains of table salt because they dissolve easier.

Massage the carrot strips and salt together to bring some of the carrots' natural water to the surface. It's hard to massage enough water out of a root vegetable, so don't lose any that comes out. After five minutes or so of massaging the carrot strips, repack them into the canning jar along with all the liquid they released and any salt that has fallen off. If there isn't enough liquid to cover the top tips of the carrots, add enough filtered water to the jar to do so.

If you have one of the fancy fermenting lids like I mentioned above, attach that now. If not, add a clean weight to the jar to hold the carrots below the liquid. Round, glass weights designed to fit wide-mouth jars are available online. Finish the fermentation jar by loosely attaching a one- or two-piece lid. The lid must be loose enough to allow the carbon dioxide gas produced by the fermentation process to escape, or else your jar may explode.

Leave the jar on your countertop for a few weeks for the fermentation to be completed. A day or two after starting the fermentation, you should observe bubbles begin to form in the brine. You can begin to taste the pickles after a couple of weeks. If they taste fine to you, they are done. If you'd like them a little sourer, leave them to ferment longer. The taste is totally up to you. Once the carrots are perfect, move the jar to your refrigerator to retard any further fermentation.

If you used a fancy fermenting lid, replace it with a regular lid. If you want to make the pickles shelf-stable, you'll need to process them in boiling water for about forty-five minutes. Unless you are making a large quantity that won't reasonably fit in in your fridge, or you are planning to give the pickled carrots as gifts, I wouldn't go to the extra effort to process the carrots. You can easily pickle other root vegetables this way. I can't think of a vegetable I wouldn't try. Thin-leaf vegetables such as spinach may not be strong enough, but just about anything else that is pulled out of the ground with work.

Miso fermentation

If the method I just described for fermenting the carrots seems too complicated, consider a Japanese method used to make *misozuke*. These are pickles produced by immersing the item to pickled in miso, a fermented soy-bean paste. Most miso pastes are about 9% salt, more than enough to ferment whatever is placed in it.

Using miso, I've pickled radishes, endive, cucumbers, carrots, scallops, oysters, prawns, and eggs. The fermentation time has varied from three days for the shellfish to two weeks for eggs to one week for radishes to thirteen weeks for the endive.

My preference is to use *shiro* (white) miso because its flavour is milder than the darker miso pastes. Although I prefer Japanese brands, you may only find local brands at your nearby health-food store. If you are fortunate enough to live in an area that carries Asian, or better yet Japanese, products obtaining miso should not be a problem.

Although you can easily pickle carrots cut into sticks, as described earlier, I think small carrots with their exteriors intact are best to use. It's even more fun if you can find small carrots in a variety of colours for these pickles. The colours become muted during the fermentation process, but they still should be recognizable. I trim the carrot stalks, if they are present down to about 6 mm (¼ in) long. Any brown ones are removed, and any dirt or discoloured area in the collar are scraped out with the tip of a paring knife. Alternatively, the entire crown could be trimmed off.

To ferment carrots with miso, place the carrots in a plastic bag that has some type of air-tight closure. Add a large spoonful or two of miso to the bag. Massage the miso around the carrots so that the carrots are mostly coated with the miso. Squeeze the carrots and miso into a lump inside the bag, expel as much air as you can from the bag, and seal the bag. Place the bag on a shelf in your refrigerator where you'll see it each day. I usually position the bag so the opening is up in case there's a leak.

If you don't want to do your fermentation in plastic, a covered, rectangular glass or ceramic bowl could be used. You'll probably need a bit more miso to keep the carrots totally submerged in the miso. Don't be afraid to use your fingers, assuming they were washed after you changed the oil on your car, to mix the carrots and miso.

Each day for the first week, give the bag a quick massage, regroup the carrots, and return in it your refrigerator. If using a hard container, give the carrots and miso a quick mix with your fingers. After a day or two, you'll notice that the miso is no longer a paste, but has become diluted with water being expelled by the carrots. After a week of fermenting, taste one of the carrots. If it's not yet to your liking, return the bag to your fridge a little longer.

Once the miso fermented carrots are ready, rinse them well in cold water and dry on paper towels. My preferred way of storing miso fermented pickles is to vacuum pack them. The easiest place for me to store mine is in my refrigerator, so there they go. I've left them at room temperature when I travelled with fermented carrots, but I've always refrigerated them when I reached my destination. So far, no one I know has gotten sick on the pickles with frequent-flyer miles.

Acid fermentation

Acid fermentation is what more people think of when they hear the word pickle. For my entire childhood, I only knew of four types of pickles: kosher dills, bread and butter pickles, pickle relish, and pickled herring. If someone offered me a pickle, I expected a kosher dill. More than likely, if the pickle came from a jar, the label said Heinz on it. Once in a while my mother procured a pickle or two from a local deli. Those were the best.

I never thought about making my own pickles of this type until a friend gave me a recipe she found in a cooking magazine. The time coincided with the time when pickling cucumbers first appeared at my corner market. That was about twenty years ago. Every year since then I make some variety of the recipe at least once a summer.

The basic concept of acid fermented pickles is quite simple. Create a brine with an acidity of about 2.5%, add the item to be pickled along with whatever else you want, seal the jar, and wait until the pickles are ready. The acidity is easy to reach since most vinegars have their acidity displayed on their labels and tend to range between 5% and 6%. To get close to the ideal acidity, it is only necessary to dilute the vinegar by half with water.

Typical recipes also called for the addition of a little salt. I suspect that because the salt concentration is so low, the salt was added more for seasoning than to encourage lactic-acid fermentation.

Older pickle recipes often called for pasteurization and pressure canning of the pickles to make them shelf stable. The pasteurization killed the bacteria present on the pickle ingredients. The pressure canning was performed to eliminate any botulism spores that may have been present and would have multiplied in the anaerobic condition created if the pickles were canned after only undergoing water processing. With our large, modern refrigerators, those steps are no longer necessary.

Since pasteurization involves cooking the pickles in their liquid mixture, further treatment was required to prevent the main player, usually cucumbers from becoming soft and mushy. The solution was to use pickling lime, calcium hydroxide, to crosslink the pectin in the cucumbers. After a twenty-four soak in a 5% lime solution, cucumbers could be boiled for hours without losing their crispness. The pectin is a polysaccharide, which is a long chain of glucose molecules. When polysaccharides crosslink, they can form incredibly strong gels. With cucumbers, we have lots of the crispiness that people expect in a pickle.

The simplest method for making carrot pickles is to mix white spirit vinegar 50-50 with filtered water. To determine how much pickling liquid you'll need, first prepare the carrots and pack them into your canning jar. Fill the jar with filtered water until the water reaches the top. If you are using a glass weight or similar device to hold the carrots in the pickling liquid, add that to the jar also. Next, carefully pour the water into a measuring cup. The amount of liquid in the cup should be a little more than the final amount of pickling liquid you'll need in the end. If you only used tap water to do the measurement, rinse and drain to minimize any minerals left from the tap water. To make your calculations simpler, round your pickling liquid volume up to a convenient amount, then throw away half the water and make up to the original volume with white vinegar.

Use filtered water because if there's too much calcium in the water, the pickles may become tough. Add about a tablespoon of table salt for each 500 ml (2 cups) of pickling liquid. Combine the liquid with carrot spears in a jar with a glass weight on the carrot spears so that they remain submerged. Place the jar in the back of your refrigerator. Tape a note as to when the pickling started to the refrigerator door. After about ten days to two weeks, check the pickles for flavour. Once ready to eat, the jar of carrot pickles is just kept in the back of your refrigerator until its contents are gone.

Variations and suggestions

I use plain, non-iodized, table salt for my pickling. Any pure salt without lots of other minerals works. I use table salt because with its fine grain size it dissolves faster than coarser salts. Many recipes call for bringing the pickling liquid to a boil to dissolve the salt and, if used, sugar. Since it takes time to bring the liquid to a boil and then to cool it down, I prefer to just zap the liquid with my immersion liquidiser to rapidly agitate the liquid and quickly dissolve the solids. A regular liquidiser would work, but that is more work to set-up and wash. I'm not worried about killing any bacteria in the water or vinegar.

If you want to make your pickles sweeter, add granulated sugar. For a true sweet and sour taste, usually the same amount of sugar is added as there is vinegar. Premixed pickling spices are available from many stores. I start with about a tablespoon of this spice per 500 ml (2 cups) of pickling liquid. Want some heat? Add some crushed, dried chili flakes. Add fresh herbs such as dill, rosemary, or thyme by the whole sprig. Garlic can be added sliced or whole in the skin. How much? Whatever feels good to you.

If you plan to hot process the carrots, first soak them for a while in a 1% pickling lime solution. Pickling lime is not very soluble, and most of the powder settles out of solution when you use it. I just mix the lime with the water in a stainless steel or glass bowl and submerge the carrots in the solution for about an hour. I do this while I'm in the kitchen doing other things so I can give the bowl a mix about every quarter hour. I use my bare hands so I can feel the carrots surface change and become tougher. I have no idea what it does to my hands. Maybe they get tougher, too. Use rubber gloves or a spoon, if your wish. When done, give your carrots a good rinse. Since the pickling lime doesn't dissolve easily, any place it has dripped will be covered with white powder. I rinse all the utensils used very thoroughly, but it's not uncommon to have to do so for a second time.

Concluding thoughts

There is no one way to make carrot pickles, and it hard to make bad batch. Play with the flavourings and the process until you arrive at one that is your favourite. My favourite is miso pickling because the process is so simple, and I like the flavour of miso. Not everyone does.

Savoury Cooked Methods
Served Cold

10 - 18

10. Blanched Carrots

Sounds boring, doesn't it? On the contrary, the process of blanching can reduce the qualities of raw carrot that some people find objectionable – its hard texture and sharp flavour – and at the same time produce a sweeter carrot flavour with a pleasing bite. Blanching is sometimes referred to as parboiling, but the processes are quite different. Blanched vegetables are boiled and then chilled whereas parboiled vegetables are boiled and then finished with other hot cooking methods.

Prepare for the blanch

Blanching is a two-step process where the carrots are first rapidly cooked by boiling, and then rapidly chilled in ice water to stop the cooking from proceeding further. The carrots can either be cut to their final size and shape before blanching or left whole for blanching and cut after blanching. The determining factors are how the carrots are to be used in the end and how good the cook's knife skills are. The cooked carrot is easier to cut for most cooks.

When blanching, choose a pot for the process that is substantially larger than the carrots to be cooked. Although the carrots only need to be covered by boiling water, there must be enough head space above the boiling liquid to allow for expansion. Likewise, a generous amount of cheap salt, about tablespoon or two per litre (quart), must be added to the water when still cool. If added to boiling water, the water rapidly expands and possibly overflows. Use cheap salt, not the expensive finishing salt you were given by your aunt last Christmas.

Water with significant amounts of calcium and magnesium may have a negative effect on blanched foods. If your tap water is hard or contains a perceived amount of chlorine, cook with filtered water. Not doing so may have no negative effect, but it can also leave the blanched vegetables hard in texture and faded in colour. The quality of the ice water is less important.

Besides a pot, you'll also need a small knife with a sharp tip. A typical paring knife works. The vegetable surface is pierced periodically during cooking with the knife tip to determine doneness. If you haven't tested for doneness with a knife tip in the past, check one or two carrot pieces every minute or so while they are cooking so you can feel the transition from raw to cooked. By testing often, you'll learn how to make the judgement. In the end, you want the carrot to allow the tip of the knife to smoothly pierce the cooked carrot, but not slide in without resistance.

While the carrots are cooking, prepare your water-ice bath. This is nothing more than a generous quantity of water chilled with a few ice cubes. If your refrigerator has a generous ice maker, use lots of ice. If you're stuck with making ice in trays, don't sacrifice too many cubes, especially if it means missing your nightly cocktail. The cold water cools the hot carrots and the ice cubes help keep the water cool. The process is referred to as 'shocking', but it's not.

You'll need a means of moving the cooked carrots from the boiling water to the water-ice bath. You can either do this with a skimmer or slotted spoon for small quantities or for greater speed, drain the cooked vegetable into a strainer or colander. You'll also need a tool to lift individual pieces of carrot above the water surface for testing. I use tongs, but I've seen other cooks use a skimmer or spoon. It's a matter of personal preference.

Do the blanch

After assembling all the equipment you'll need for the blanching and preparing your carrots, bring your pot of salted water to a rapid boil over the highest heat you can reach on your hob. Carefully add the carrots without splashing. The water immediately starts to cool, so leave the hob on its highest setting until the water starts to boil again. The hob can then be turned down to reduce splashing, but never low enough to so the boiling visibly stops.

While the carrots are cooking, make sure the water-ice bath is prepared and the strainer or colander are nearby and handy. Start testing the cooking carrots with the tip of a knife as described above.

When the carrots seem almost cooked — remember that they continue to cook for a short time in the cold water — quickly drain through the colander or the strainer and add to the water-ice bath. The carrots do not have to be dry before plunging them into the cooling liquid. Depending on the size of carrots, it may take ten to fifteen minutes to reduce the interior temperature low enough to stop cooking.

When cool, drain the carrots on kitchen paper. If the carrots still need to be cut, do so now. The cooked, almost dry carrots can be stored in your refrigerator in a covered container until needed.

Finish the carrots

Blanched carrots are great to eat with a dipping sauce. Salad dressings also work great. You choose which to try. I'm too lazy to dip so I'll cut the carrots into shreds and serve them as a dressed salad. (See 15. Carrot Salad, page 83) Some people like them served with simply a nice finishing salt. You can eat the blanched carrots as is or as a base for another preparation. What you do with them is both a matter of mood and creativity.

11. Carrot Foam

One of the most popular desserts or snacks in Switzerland is a cold, baked meringue served with triple cream. The meringue is nothing more than egg white and sugar whipped into a very stiff foam and until the sugar is fully dissolved. The foam is baked at a low temperature for a long time to fully dehydrate it without it losing its shape.

Unlike egg whites, which have lots of protein to crosslink and trap gas, carrots are mostly cellulose. Just combining carrots with sugar will not create a foam, no matter how much it is whipped. A carrot foam can be created by adding a small amount of methylcellulose made from cellulose pulp taken from plant cell walls. One commercial methylcellulose, Methocel F50, allows a somewhat stable foam to be created from carrot juice and sugar. By baking or dehydrating the foam, it can be made into a stable snack.

The raw quantities in this recipe produce about sixteen, amuse-bouche-

sized portions. The actual quantity of finished 'crackers' is relative to how large you make them and how many you consider successful.

> 250 ml (8½ fl oz) strained carrot juice
> 40 g (1¼ oz) finely granulated sugar
> 9 g (¼ oz) methylcellulose (Methocel F50)

Combine the juice and sugar in the bowl of a stand mixer. Using a stick liquidiser, agitate the juice until the sugar is completely dissolved. Then, sprinkle the methylcellulose over the surface, and continue agitating with the stick liquidiser until the methylcellulose is hydrated and well dispersed. Place the bowl in your refrigerator until the liquid is well chilled.

Attach the chilled bowl to the stand mixer fitted with a whisk attachment. Whisk at high speed until the foam supports medium to stiff peaks, about ten minutes.

Spread the foam evenly over the surface of a liquid-appropriate tray in a food dehydrator, or a silicone-rubber baking mat on a baking sheet. Dehydrate at 55°C (131°F) in a dehydrator or convection oven until the foam is dry and crisp, about 6 hours.

Carefully cut or break the dried foam into pieces suitable for serving.

A different foam

What the English-speaking world refers to foam, the French call *mousse* and the Spanish call *espuma*. Whipped cream might be the foam that all of us are the most familiar with. Here, you'll make a foam with the flavour of carrots and the texture of softly whipped cream.

Both raw carrot juice and filtered carrot juice works fine for this foam. The difference in the final product is dependent on your juicer. If your juicer leaves a few very small pieces of carrot in the raw juice, you'll notice these in the final foam. Whether raw or filtered juice is used, the flavour is the same.

This foam requires a bit of protein to crosslink and create the gel that captures the air. You will use gelatine to provide this protein. Unfortunately, not all gelatines are equal in their gelling strength. Depending on the brand

and the form, powdered or sheet, the bloom strength ranges from 125 to 300. The powdered gelatine I'm using in this foam has a bloom strength of 225. If your gelatine is different, you'll need to calculate a multiplier to correct the quantity. The multiplier is equal to the square root of the result of 225 divided by your bloom strength. You can approximate the multiplier from the table below. Select the bloom strength closest to yours and read the multiplier shown below it.

Bloom Strength	125	150	175	200	225	250	275	300
Multiplier	1.3	1.2	1.1	1.1	1.0	0.9	0.9	0.9

To make this foam, for a given quantity of juice, you'll need 2.2% times the multiplier of gelatine and 0.1% xanthan gum. Everything is calculated by weight.

For example, assume that you are starting with 250 ml (8½ fl oz) of carrot juice. This quantity of juice weighs close to 250 g (8⅞ oz). If you are using sheets of 'silver' gelatine, which has a bloom strength of 160, you'll require 1.2 times 0.022 times 250, or 6.6 g of gelatine. You'll also need 0.001 times 250, or 0.25 g of xanthan gum.

To serve the foam, you'll need a whipping siphon and one or two cream (nitrous oxide) chargers. To shear in the xanthan gum, you'll need an immersion or stick liquidiser.

To start, measure out the three ingredients. Place about a quarter of the juice in a saucepan. If you're using powdered gelatine, sprinkle the gelatine over the surface of the juice. If you're using sheet gelatine, submerge the sheets in the juice. Set the saucepan aside for a few minutes to allow the gelatine to soften. Place the saucepan over low heat and slowly warm the contents. The gelatine should melt when the liquid reaches 50 °C (122 °F). Do not let the temperature exceed 60 °C (140 °F), or the gelatine's setting strength may be affected.

When the gelatine is fully dissolved, remove the saucepan from the heat. Add the remaining juice and mix. Shear in the xanthan gum using your immersion liquidiser. This can also be done with vigorous whisking, but it's a lot harder and more time consuming.

Place the saucepan in a water-ice bath and chill the mixture until it becomes like a gloppy pudding. This should happen around 10 °C (50 °F). Spoon the mixture into the jar of the whipping siphon. Screw the top on and refrigerate until you're ready for the foam.

To serve, charge the whipping siphon with one charger. Enthusiastically shake the jar. Dispense a test squirt. Charge again, if required. Plate the foam.

This carrot foam makes an unusual 'sauce' for cold, poached fish and similar dishes. Surprisingly, it can also be served by itself as a small side dish.

12. Carrot Dip

Party dips go all the way back to the 1950s. Before salsa became popular as dip for corn chips, most dips started off with a white base: soured cream or mayonnaise. The '60s brought free love and yogurt to the party. When the dip had to be stiff in order to stay in the groove of a celery stick or an endive leaf, cream cheese became the base. To turn any of these traditional bases into a dip, all that is required is the addition of a flavouring.

The combinations

There are many forms of carrot that can be added to a white base to make a good dip. Here are a few.

Carrot powder: Add powder to taste and allow time for the powder to hydrate before serving. Stir well to eliminate any lumps. Depending upon how much powder is added, the result can be subtle to strong. (See 47. Carrot Powder, page 177.)

Carrot pulp: Stir raw pulp into the base. Be sure to separate the pulp thoroughly when you stir. A dinner fork may do a better job than a spoon or spatula. If you use lots of pulp, it may be necessary to lighten the mixture with a little cream if it becomes too stiff. (See 2. Carrot Juice, page 42.)

Carrot juice: Because it thins the base, care must be taken when adding juice. (See 2. Carrot Juice, page 42.)

Carrot purée: Either raw or cooked, carrot purée produces a similar result to carrot pulp except it is much easier to mix with the base. (See

48. Carrot Purée, page 179.)

With four bases and four flavourings, that's sixteen different dips without breaking a sweat. Any dip made as above can be further enhanced with a spritz of salt, black pepper, or whatever else you have in your cabinet. I like a little hot sauce or dried fenugreek leaves.

13. Carrot Crackers

There are many names given to various flatbreads made to be eaten in one or two bites and cooked dry, dry enough as to not stale in a reasonable amount of time. In some ways, a dry climate is more important than how dry, within limits, the item is itself. Once the water level is low enough not to support bacteria, these biscuits or crackers last a lifetime, unless they happen to pick up moisture from the air, as happens in humid climates.

Given that cracker-like flat breads go back millennium, there should be common elements that can be built upon to make a carrot version. There are! Flour and water! The same basic dough components of pasta can be used to make a cracker. Bake very thin pieces of pasta dough at high heat, and you'll have crackers.

Making the crackers

To finely grate the carrot called for below, use a grater that produces thin, flat pieces rather than ones with a thick cross-section. These graters are usually designed for hard cheese or chocolate. Alternately, if you have any of the carrot pulp remaining from juicing carrots, that would work, too. With the pulp, you'll need to use a lot of care to disperse the pulp into the dough, but it can be done.

The following ingredient quantities produce a decent handful – I have big hands – of crackers. The actual quantity is dependent on how thin and how large you make the crackers. (And how many you snack on.)

> 75 g (½ cup) plain flour
> 75 g (½ cup) fine semolina flour

77

3 g (1 tsp) fine salt
20 g (1½ tbsp) olive oil
20 g (¾ oz) thinly grated carrot, or carrot pulp (see 2. Carrot Juice,
page 42)
60 ml (¼ cup) carrot juice
semi-coarse (0.6 to 1.2 mm grain size) salt (optional)

Using a deep bowl, combine the flours and the salt with a dinner fork. Drizzle the oil over the mixture and combine everything by pressing the oil into the flour with the back of the fork. When the oil is incorporated, mix in the carrot and continue to mix with the fork by pressing it through the mixture. Finally, add the carrot juice and continue mixing.

When well mixed, start kneading the dough in the same bowl until it comes together. Once that happens, transfer the dough to a board to make the kneading easier. When the dough can be formed into a ball, divide it into four pieces and return it to the bowl. Cover the dough with a slightly damp piece of kitchen paper.

The dough needs to be rolled to about 1 mm (½₂ in) in thickness or even less. The easiest way to accomplish this is with a pasta roller. I use one that attaches to my stand mixer, but the hand-operated versions that clamp to a table work just as well.

Preheat your oven to 200 °C (390 °F).

Using the plain rollers of the pasta machine set at their thickest setting, flatten one small dough ball and run it through the rollers several times. The dough may fall apart the first few times, but as it becomes better hydrated by the kneading produced by the rollers, it begins to hold together. Fold the dough each time it goes through the rollers. Once you produce a smooth ribbon of dough, start reducing the space between the rollers, one setting at a time.

When a thin ribbon of dough is produced, lay it flat on a baking sheet lined with greaseproof paper or a silicone-rubber baking mat. Evenly sprinkle the crackers with some coarse salt. The density is up to you. Gently press the salt into the surface of the dough. Cut the dough crosswise into strips with a pizza wheel. The width is also up to you. The pieces can be touching when they go into the oven. They shrink during cooking.

(I use a silicone-rubber baking mat right on my countertop, near the edge. After the coarse salt is sprinkled on, I use my straight rolling pin with only its own weight applied to press the salt into the dough. The mat is then carefully lifted and slid onto the baking sheet.)

The time difference between a properly baked cracker and an overcooked one is a matter of seconds. Working in small batches, start at about seven minutes of baking until your proper time is determined.

While the first crackers are baking, roll out another piece of dough and get it ready on a baking sheet. When the first batch is cooked, promptly remove it from your oven. Transfer the crackers to a cooking rack. They continue to get crispier as they cool. Once cool, store the crackers in an airtight container. They absorb moisture if left in a humid area.

A few variations

In addition to, or instead of, the coarse salt, other spices can be sprinkled over the crackers before baking. I like chipotle pepper powder. Za'atar also works, but it can burn if left too long in the oven. Dried fenugreek leaves can also be good, but they need to be added to the dough when mixing since they are reluctant to stay on top of the crackers if just sprinkled over the top.

14. Carrot Spread

In 1997, I experienced for the first time a piece of crusty bread slathered with *rillettes d'lapin*. Rillettes are the traditional French version of potted meat. The meat is cooked to the point where it easily shreds. It is then cooled and packed in fat to preserve it. When served, the meat is served with the fat that clings to it, usually on thick pieces of rustic bread.

What's in your fat?

Since carrots won't release their own, non-existing fat when cooked, we'll need to add fat to them. The choice here is whether to choose a fat that is liquid or solid at room temperature. Animal fats tend to be solid, vegetable fats tend to be liquid. The prominent exception is hydrogenated vegetable fat in the form of vegetable shortening, which I would avoid because it lacks flavour. My favourite animal fat is foie gras fat, but that is not readily available, so I use my next favourite animal fat: butter.

For vegetable fat, olive oil is the most accessible, but nut oils can be quite nice, albeit a bit more expensive. I find the smell of some olive oils too strong for my liking. They are inappropriate for a carrot spread.

Who's your carrot?

Carrots don't have the right structure or composition to shred after cooking like meat does. Furthermore, large chunks of raw carrot are a bit disconcerting in a spread, but small pieces are fine. For the spread, we can start with fresh carrot pulp leftover from juicing (see 2. Carrot Juice, page 42), which is made of very small pieces. If that is not available, blanch your carrots (see 10. Blanched Carrots, page 69) until cooked but still the smallest bit crunchy. Grate or shred the carrots once they are cooled. If they seem a bit wet, sop up any loose water with kitchen paper.

Gentlemen, start your spread

The spread, if made with a solid fat, should consist of about equal parts carrot and fat. The fat is usually at room temperature to facilitate mixing. The two items are just stirred and folded with a dinner fork until well homogenized. If made with liquid fat, the fat should simply coat the carrots. The carrots should not be swimming in the fat. Start by adding some fat to the carrots, mix the two together, and test the mixture to determine if it is moist enough. If not, add more oil.

Add more flavour

At a minimum, the carrot spread should need a little salt at this time, but there are many other flavours that can be added to provides a second

level of flavour. Dried herbs such as basil or oregano, dried flavourings such as sumac or chili peppers, and flavouring mixtures such curry powder or garum marsala can all be added to taste. Most spices probably require some time to hydrate and blend into the spread.

The flavour of the bread modifies the overall effect of the spread. A dark bread filled with nuts produces a different overall flavour than a light, buttery brioche. Instead of bread, try crackers or pieces of flat bread. In order to fulfil their initial promise, spreads must be spread onto something other than just a spoon.

Throw a wrench in the works

As an alternative to pure fat, replace that part of the spread with cream cheese or one of its cousins like mascarpone, crème fraîche, or fromage blanc. Depending on the substitute fat chosen and how loose it is, it may need a light lightening before mixing. This can usually be accomplished by simply stirring rapidly. If that doesn't work, a little cream can be beaten into the cheese to make it more mixable.

A slight alternative

A quick spread can be prepared by combining carrot purée (see 48. Carrot Purée, page 179) with an equal amount of soft, unsalted butter. (This is quick if you already have the purée on hand!)

At first, when the two ingredients are mixed, they are quite immiscible, but if you give the mixture a chance it comes together. Keep stirring until the mixture is smooth and homogenous. Taste it. A little salt may be in order. It's up to you. I like to add ground cinnamon and spread the result on wholemeal toast.

15. Carrot Salad

In its most basic form, a salad is a dish of raw or cooked vegetables with a sauce or dressing. The earlier carrot slaw (see 6. Carrot Slaw, page 53) was a much different salad based on raw carrots with minimal change to their texture and flavour. This carrot salad is based on carrots cooked until their crunch and bitterness are gone.

For carrot salad, I'd estimate starting with about 150 g (⅓ lb) of carrots per side-dish serving. The salad lasts well so it's better to make too much rather than too little.

Preparing the carrots

Cook pared carrots as described in 10. Blanched Carrots, page 69. The cooked carrots need to be rid of their crunch, but not be soft and fragile. After chilling, slice the carrots into a roll cut or into 4 to 5 cm (1¾ to 2 in) long diagonal slices. See General Information, pages 27 to 32 for slicing guidance. Set the cut carrots aside until needed.

Preparing the dressing, or not

Like with green salad, you can make your own dressing or use one from a bottle. I think fresh is both easy and more fun. It's a chance to raid the larder for scraps of things like old, dried herbs, that can be added.

Unless the carrots are too soft, as in overcooked, I like to mix the dressing ingredients in the bowl with the carrots. In this manner, each ingredient is given a chance to bind with the previous ingredients and the carrots, in order.

Mayonnaise, the first

My wife's family's potato salad dressing consists mostly of mayonnaise with a small amount of (American) salad or yellow mustard, salt, pepper, finely diced yellow onion, and finely diced celery. My mother-in-law would also add canned tuna or imitation crab, but I eschew those additions. For the carrot salad, you could just use the first four ingredients or add the onion and celery or change up whatever you wish. The dressing is mostly mayonnaise with everything else added to taste. With a little practice, you be able to add everything just by sight. If you want a dry salad, start with less mayonnaise. If you want the salad swimming in dressing, dump the whole jar on. The choice is yours.

Mayonnaise, the second

My family's salad dressing was what my mother referred to as 'Louie Dressing' and was made mainly from mayonnaise, tomato catsup, salt, and pepper. Using a catsup to mayonnaise ratio of one-to-three or four, this works fine for carrot salad. My brother likes to add hot curry powder to the mix. I prefer to add horseradish, Worcestershire sauce, Mexican-style chili sauce, and sweet pickle relish. The whole shebang is up to you but the comments from above may apply.

Oil, the first

I've always prepared a somewhat non-standard vinegar and oil salad dressing, and it works for carrots. To start, add salt and pepper to the carrots, and mix. Sprinkle enough oil – olive, almond, walnut, hazelnut, etc. – on the carrots so they just glisten. The bottom of the bowl should still be dry. Sprinkle a little vinegar – red wine, champagne, raspberry, honey, or other type of vinegar – over the carrots. Start with just a little, and after mixing, taste the results. Add more if you'd like. If you want to bump the dressing up a bit, add some finely minced fresh or dried herbs. If dried herbs are used, allow some time for them to hydrate – test by tasting – before serving the salad.

Oil, the second

If you want more of a swimming dressing, add enough olive oil so there's a little wading pool in the bottom of the bowl. Add an herb-based combination, such as za'atar in a generous amount. Mix everything well. Depending on you herb blend, a little more salt may be needed. Try your salad and see. As the herb blend is hydrating, it may settle. Be sure to give your salad a good mix before serving.

16. Carrot Leather

Fruit leather is a form of dried fruit made from a purée rather than whole fruit. The puréed fruit is cooked, sometimes with added sugar, and then dried in thin sheets. Carrots may not be fruit, but they contain significant sugar and are high in pectin, a common gelling agent.

Basic issues

The ingredients of carrot leather are peeled carrots, granulated sugar, lemon juice, and water. A piece of leather similar in size to a quarter-sized sheet pan – about 23 by 33 cm (9 by 13 in) – accommodates about 300 g (10½ oz) of carrots. Sugar is added at a rate of 10% and lemon juice at 5% of the weight of the carrots. Therefore, multiply the carrot weight by 0.1 and 0.05 to determine the two weights.

Making the purée

Finely grate or shred pared carrots. They should feel damp, which is good. Weigh the carrots and calculate the amount of sugar and lemon juice required. Place the carrots in a covered saucepan over low heat. Add the sugar and lemon juice. Slowly bring the carrots to heat so the small amount of liquid in the bottom of the pan is bubbling. Stir often, scrapping the bottom of the pan so the mixture doesn't burn.

After the carrots collapse a bit and the saucepan seems less full, add enough water to almost come to the top of the carrots. Simmer the mixture over low heat until the carrots lose their crunchiness and seem cooked.

Transfer the mixture to the bowl of food processor fitted with a standard cutting blade. Process the carrot mixture into a smooth purée. It may be necessary to add a little more water. The final product must be smooth and easily spreadable without being runny. If too thick, add more water. If too thin, which is unlikely, transfer the mixture back into the saucepan and cook over low heat, uncovered, until thicker.

Tanning the leather

Prepare your sheet pans by covering the food surface with a single layer of cling film. Alternately, simply oil the metal surface lightly with a neutral vegetable oil. The cling film can be a pain to keep in place initially, but the oiled surface leaves a slight oily film on the finished leather.

Pour the purée into the centre of a prepared pan. Using a large offset spatula, spread the purée into an even layer, about 3 to 6 mm (⅛ to ¼ in) thick.

The purée is turned into leather by slowly drying the mixture. This can be accomplished in a dehydrator or an oven. You'll want the temperature set to 60 °C (140 °F) or as close to that as possible. If you are using an oven and it has a convection fan, turn that on. If not, prop the oven door open slightly with a thick towel so moisture isn't trapped in the oven.

Dry the purée until the surface is no longer tacky and it looks a bit rough. The purée noticeably shrinks while it is drying. If the leather is only dried partway through its thickness, turn it over, discarding the cling film. The purée may crack if it dries too fast, but the effect is that the leather appears more rustic.

Store the dried leather in a sealed plastic bag or container. If the leather meets moisture, or even humid weather, it may get sticky.

17. Carrot Terrine

Vegetable terrines are a staple of mid-century nouvelle cuisine. Most contained a panoply of vegetables floating in a gelatinized cream, sometimes further filled with diced mushroom or fresh herbs. For this terrine, we move from multiplicity to singularity. The only vegetable used is a carrot. (No surprise there!)

Determine your equipment

Since this dish is called a terrine, you'll need one. In French, a terrine is a deep ceramic bowl in either a round, oval, or rectangular shape. For this preparation, use a rectangular terrine so the carrots neatly stack. If one isn't available, a small loaf pan makes a nice substitute. The ingredient quantities specified in this description are appropriate for a 450 g (1 lb) terrine. The weight represents the contents, not the terrine itself. You can determine the terrine size by weighing the water that it holds without overflowing.

Also helpful in the preparation of this terrine is a small, about 30 ml (2 tbsp), ladle. Besides being convenient for transferring the liquid filler, the bottom of the ladle is convenient for spreading the filler liquid into an even layer.

Preparing the carrots

Pare and blanch (see 10. Blanched Carrots, page 69) the carrots. There should be enough carrots to neatly half-fill the terrine with the carrots sitting parallel to the long dimension of the terrine. Of course, it never hurts to have a little extra. After blanching, slice the carrots lengthwise into wedges. A big carrot may produce eight wedges whereas a medium one may produce four and a skinny carrot is left uncut. Your goal is to have a bunch of carrot pieces that appear to have the same cross-sectional size. The carrot pieces should be long enough to almost touch both ends of the terrine. Short pieces can be butted together.

Set the carrot pieces on a plate lined with kitchen paper and chill until the carrots are needed.

Preparing the filler

The filler should be prepared just before it is needed. If it gels solid, it can be liquified again, but it is better not too. For the terrine discussed above, you'll need about 300 ml (1¼ cups) of cream. Use a cream with greater than 36% butterfat, but one that still flows easily. In the United Kingdom, that's double cream whereas in the United States, that's heavy cream or manufacturer's cream. Avoid using 'ultra-pasteurized' cream because of its slightly metallic taste. To thicken this much cream, you'll need 12 g of gelatine (160 bloom strength), leaf or granules. If you have a different bloom strength gelatine, use the chart in 11. Carrot Foam, page 71, to determine how to correct the gelatine quantity. Or you can ignore the difference and chance that the filler may be a little stiff. You'll also need some fine salt and

finely ground white pepper.

Place the cream in a saucepan. If using gelatine granules, sprinkle them over the surface of the cream. When the granules have swollen, place the cream over low heat, and warm it enough to melt the gelatine. If using leaves of gelatine, place them in a glass of cold water to soften. Place the saucepan over low heat, and warm the cream. When soft, drain the gelatine, squeeze out the water, and add it to the warm cream and stir until the gelatine is no longer visible. Salt and pepper the cream to taste.

Set the saucepan aside, but do not refrigerate.

Filling the terrine

Ladle enough cream into the terrine to seriously coat the bottom. Set the terrine in your refrigerator.

When the bottom coating is gelled, remove the terrine from your refrigerator. Arrange a layer of cooked and chilled carrots over the bottom layer of gelled cream. Allow a lateral space of about 5 mm (¼ in) between each piece and between the pieces and the sides of the terrine. Ladle enough cream into the terrine to cover the carrots. Set the terrine in your refrigerator.

When the cream covering the carrots is gelled, remove the terrine from your refrigerator. Arrange another layer of carrots, cover with cream, and chill as above. Continue alternating cream and carrots, ending with a layer of cream at the top of the terrine. If the cream becomes too thick, heat it gently until fluid. Do not heat it more than is necessary to barely liquify it.

If the terrine has a lid, place it in place. Otherwise, cover the terrine with cling film. Return the terrine to your refrigerator until thoroughly chilled, at least eight hours.

Unmoulding the terrine

A few hours before serving, remove the terrine from the refrigerator. Gently pull the gelled cream slightly from sides of the terrine. Place a generous piece of cling film on a flat surface. Gently unmould the terrine by turning it upside down shaking it gently. Sometimes working on just one side gets air into the bottom of the terrine to release block of cream. As a last resort, place the terrine in a deep pan of warm water to melt the outer surface. Try to avoid doing this.

Once the terrine is released onto the cling film, wrap the block so the sides are enclosed in unwrinkled film. Fold the excess film over the ends. Place the block onto a plate, and chill it until serving time.

Serving the terrine

Place the chilled block of carrots and cream on a very flat cutting board. Using a thin slicing knife, trim off the ends of the terrine. Snack on the trimmings. Carefully cut the terrine, through the cling film, into even slices. Be sure to slice. Do not simply push the knife down – the terrine will collapse – slice. As you cut each slice, transfer it to a chilled plate. Carefully remove the cling film from the slice.

Serve the terrine as a first course as is, or with a hot and sour carrot sauce (see 43. Carrot Sauce, page 169). The sauce can be spooned onto the plate before the terrine slice is positioned or drizzled over it. The plates can be made up ahead of time and chilled until service.

Savoury Cooked Methods
Served Hot

18 - 33

18. Sous-vide Carrots

Sous-vide cooking has been popular in restaurants for a couple of decades. Even though it was only introduced in the 1980s to cook-and-chill commercial foods, the concept dates to Charles Dickens' discussion of temperature-limited cooking in an 1854 edition of his *Weekly Journal*. Most sous-vide cooking could be termed temperature-limited cooking because the final cooking temperature of the food item is limited by the temperature of the water bath. Once the internal temperature of the food matches that of the water, the food can be left in the water for quite a while longer without overcooking. The exception to this is the cooking of eggs where both time and temperature are used to determine the cooking procedure. If left past the determined cook time, the eggs can overcook.

Modern, sous-vide cooking

The modern, home version of this technique is accomplished by packaging the food to be cooked in a plastic bag and placing the bag in water at a set temperature for a pre-determined period of time. The water is held at a constant temperature by either using a special container with its own temperature maintenance system or any container with a device that circulates the water and holds it at the desired temperature. These 'circulators', the basis of the later method, have become inexpensive enough for most households to afford.

Why sous-vide cooking works

The common methods of cooking vegetables with heat all achieve their results by raising the vegetable's internal temperature to above 85 °C (185 °F), the temperature where cellulose – the major structural component in vegetables – begins to break down and the vegetable is declared tender. Most methods do this quickly with a higher than required temperature where there's a chance of overcooking the vegetables. By using a temperature-limited method, the chance of producing a mushy, overcooked result are greatly reduced.

Set up your equipment

There are three common categories of equipment available to the home cook for temperature-limited cooking: water ovens, circulators, and regulated hobs. Water ovens were the first piece of equipment available for home cooks. They take the longest time to set up and come to temperature. Circulators have gone through several generations and from being more than twice the price of water ovens to less than one-third. The market is now swimming in the different versions available. The third option, temperature regulated hobs, combine a freestanding induction hob with a feedback mechanism to maintain the pot contents at a constant temperature. This option can be used like a water oven, but since the attached pot is easily cleaned, no plastic packaging is required. These hobs are also the most expensive approach to temperature-limited cooking.

Choose your bag

If you have one of the vacuum packaging systems commonly used with temperature-limited cooking, then I recommend using that over the second option of using a zipper-sealed bag. If the second option is chosen, the safety of the bag at high temperature must be verified with the manufacturer. The air in the bag must be removed by carefully lowering the bag and its contents into a basin of water with only the bag opening above the water level. As you coax all the air from the bag, simultaneously seal the zipper closure. Any air bubbles left in the bag expand when heated, causing the bag to float. Some cooks add a weight, such as a dinner knife, to the bag. Any water trapped in the process may turn to vapour, which also expands the bag. The food doesn't cook well if it is inside a pillow! Home vacuum packaging systems can be inexpensive and useful for things other than temperature-limited cooking.

Prepare your carrots

How I prepare a carrot for temperature-limited cooking can vary from simply providing a good washing to a fancy paring and a stately trim. How you prepare your carrots is up to you. If you check online resources, you'll find that some people like to split fat carrots lengthwise into two pieces for more even cooking. Sometimes I do and sometimes I don't. Recently, I've seen bags of multi-coloured carrots in grocery stores. Low temperature cooking tends to intensify the colour of the vegetable being cooked, so these carrots should look very attractive on your dinner plate.

Either salt the carrots before or after cooking. My preference is before cooking. A sprinkle with table salt is enough. Expensive, fancy salt won't bring out the carrots' flavour any better than the cheap stuff. If you want to add some herbs or fat, butter or olive oil, to the bag for cooking, prepare these now.

Finally, choose your method of bagging from the descriptions above. Bag the carrots in a single layer along with any herbs or fat.

Cook your carrots

When cooking items such as meat at lower temperatures for a longer time period I don't bother to preheat the water, but in this case, it is important to preheat since, depending on your system, the preheat time may be longer than the cooking time. When the water reaches 85 °C (185 °F), add the plastic bag with the carrots to the hot water. Be sure that there is ample, at least 1 cm (⅜ in), water around all sides of the bag. This is to prevent cooler, slower cooking areas from occurring.

The total cooking time is a matter of how large the carrots are and how well done you desire the outcome. The time may be as short as ten minutes for thin carrots cooked tender-crisp to a full hour for fatter, more cooked carrots. Using tongs or long cooking tweezers, periodically remove the bag from the hot water and test a couple of carrots by pressing firmly with your fingers. If you do it quickly, you won't burn yourself.

If the serving time is still a way off, the carrots in their bag can be held in a warm 70 °C (160 °F) oven or in 60 °C (140 °F) water.

Serving

Open the bag with scissors, or if appropriate, zip it open. Slide the carrots onto

97

the serving plates. If the carrots were cooked in fat, drizzle a little of that over the carrots. If not done earlier, sprinkle the carrots with fine salt, or if a different texture is desired, sprinkle the carrots with a finishing salt. Serve very hot.

19. Roast Carrots

Native Americans roasted unhusked corn directly in the coals of a fire. It's hard for me to not imagine any indigenous people not roasting any whole, solid vegetable with a significant skin or covering in a fire. Today, you can find many recipes online to roast potatoes and corn on your grill. Whether ancient or recent, baking whole vegetables by direct heat has always been independent of the cook having an oven.

First, take an oven

Today, you'd have to be born at the end of the Great Depression to remember a time when not all homes and apartments had ovens, and those that did often had ovens that were less than stellar. Even modern ovens can be wildly out of calibration, require long time periods to preheat, have inconsistent temperatures throughout their volume, or have wide swings in temperature during the cooking cycle. Recipes have attempted to mitigate these deficiencies by instructing the reader where in the oven to place a baking sheet or to turn the baking sheet part of the way through the cooking.

The switch to electric ovens, which began in the 1920s and became almost complete after the end of the Second World War, meant that restaurant ovens didn't need to be left on all day. It also meant that temperature regulation for both home and commercial ovens became less an art and more a matter of setting a dial.

All these factoids aside, it is still amazing that it might be less than fifty years since roasted vegetables became ubiquitous on restaurant menus. Some researchers credit the first roasted vegetables to a restaurant called Al Forno, which opened in Providence, Rhode Island, in 1980. As the name implies, *al forno* means 'baked' in Italian, everything was cooked in the

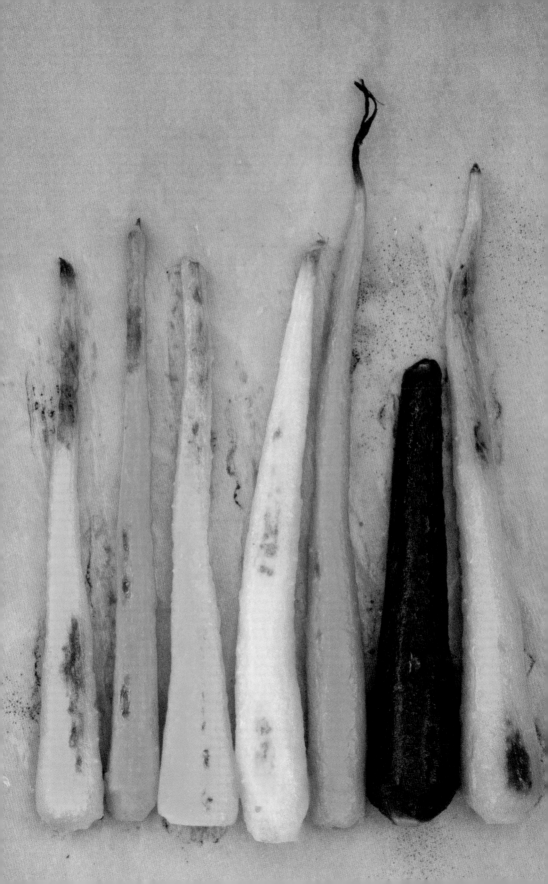

oven. Apparently, their first successful roast vegetable was asparagus. It is now common to roast almost any vegetable.

Second, turn the oven on

Why say 'roast vegetables' instead of 'baked vegetables'? I have concluded that the preferred term is one of convention, and that no other consistent definition exists. I've heard cooking teachers say that baking refers to sweet products and roasting refers to savoury products, and yet we say 'baked potatoes' when we cook potatoes whole with their skins intact in the oven (at least we do when they are not being referred to as 'jacket potatoes') and 'roast potatoes' when we cook them peeled and cut-up. We bake a meatloaf, but roast a leg of lamb.

Whereas ovens during the twentieth century only had a 'bake' setting, modern ovens may have a 'roast' setting in addition to the 'bake' setting. The advent of these settings corresponded to when the electric elements were moved from being inside the oven box to its outside. With the 'bake' setting, the oven is heated only from the bottom. With the 'roast' setting, the oven is heated from both the top and bottom. Now, instead of using the 'bake' setting when roasting our leg of lamb, we use the 'roast' setting. The effect on the finished dish is that the meat develops a crust faster, even though the temperature is still set the same.

Now that we have modern ovens that truly reach high temperatures, why aren't vegetables roasted more often at home? Over my years of teaching I've heard many reasons, from 'I don't know how to' to 'I don't know how to turn my oven on', and from 'It makes too much of a mess' to 'It takes too long.' All these reasons are unfortunate because roasting produces very tasty vegetables. When properly cooked, roast vegetables have an agreeable brown crust and property cooked interiors.

Why do carrots brown on the outside?

The brown crust is really two types of non-enzymatic browning and is relative to the components of the vegetables and the application of heat.

Caramelisation is a poorly understood reaction that produces hundreds of nutty flavours by subjecting the sugars in the vegetable to pyrolysis. Carrots contain the sugars glucose, fructose, and sucrose. Three-quarters of the sugar is glucose and the remainder is almost equally divided between the other two sugars. At a neutral pH, the fructose begins to caramelise at 110 °C (230 °F) and the other two sugars begin to caramelise at 160 °C (320 °F). Since the last two sugars make up almost 90% of the sugar in a carrot, they dominate the non-enzymatic browning due to caramelisation.

The second type of non-enzymatic browning that occurs with roasted vegetables is the Maillard reaction, which is named after the French chemist who first described it in 1912. This browning happens mostly at a lower temperature, 140 to 165 °C (284 to 329 °F), and thus precedes some browning due to caramelisation. The Maillard reaction is a chemical reaction between amino acids and reducing sugars. In carrots, the reducing sugars are the monosaccharides fructose and glucose, which make up almost 90% of the sugar in carrots. The amino acid in carrots that the reducing sugars most like to react with is lysine, which constitutes about 5% of the amino acids present.

Why don't carrots brown on the inside?

From the above we can see that there is a wide range of temperatures that we can roast carrots at to achieve a browning effect on the surface. Why not all the way through the carrot? Remember that the carrot consists mostly of water. Water boils at a temperature of 100 °C (212 °F) or lower, depending on your elevation. It takes about thirty-five times more energy to turn the liquid water in a cell into steam – this is referred to as change of state – then to raise the temperature of the cell one degree. As the carrot heats up and the water in the cells approaches its boiling point, the cell walls begin to fracture. This is the process of the carrot becoming tender instead of crunchy. If water is still present, because of the energy required to cause the change of state, the interior of the carrots cannot reach a browning temperature. See 21. Steamed Carrots, page 110, for further discussion about steaming carrots.

How ovens cook

To roast carrots you'll need a wide, heatproof container so you can spread the carrots into a single layer. My preferred container is a rimmed baking sheet, but you can also use a shallow baking pan or dish. Both conventional and convection ovens cook primarily by radiant heat. Radiant heat is what you feel from the sun when you are outside. To lower the heat hitting your body, you stand in the shade. In an oven, the sides of a pan act like a beach umbrella. The food in the pan takes longer to cook depending on how high the sides of the pan are. Since there is no liquid to be concerned with while roasting carrots, it is only necessary to have sides high enough to keep the carrots from rolling off the baking sheet when it is moved from your countertop to your oven and on the return trip.

To pare and trim or not

The carrots to be roasted can either be pared or not. Carrots that are not pared develop almost a peel-able skin when roasted. This makes for an interesting combination of textures in the finished dish. The carrots pieces need to be close to the same size and shape so each piece takes about the same time to cook. When roasting whole carrots, I prefer their diameter to be about 2 cm (¾ in) or less, and only washed. If you have larger carrots, they can be cut into spears of a smaller dimension. Some people cut out and discard the cores because they don't like their aftertaste, which can sometimes be bitter. I usually don't bother with this step.

The carrots don't have to be in long pieces when they are roasted. Typical supermarket carrots can be pared and then sliced diagonally into 5 cm (2 in) long by 5 mm (¼ in) thick pieces. The pieces have an oval shape of varying widths. The 'sharp' tips and edges of the pieces will cook faster, giving a more pronounced caramel taste. When roasting shapes like these, line your baking sheet with a silicone-rubber baking mat so the pieces don't stick to the baking sheet and are easier to flip part way through cooking.

The supporting actors

Beside the carrots, the other two ingredients required for the roasting are a little oil and some salt. The oil can be ordinary vegetable oil or something more exotic. The function of the oil is mostly to prevent sticking and to help the surface of the carrots develop a nice patina. Choose an oil that can handle high heat, which most refined oils can. Using an expensive extra-virgin olive oil or a fancy nut oil works, but they impart little or no flavour to the final dish. I'm conservative – and cheap – so I use a plain olive oil for roasting carrots.

Ordinary table salt is fine for roasting. The function of the salt is to bring out the flavour and sweetness of the carrots. It is not in the dish to impart a salty taste or crunchy texture. Science says that people prefer their food to be salted at a rate of about 0.5%. That would mean about a teaspoon for every 450 g (1 lb) of carrots. Some of the salt sticks to the carrots. Some of the salt stays in the mixing bowl with the excess oil. I'd start with a single three-finger pinch for that amount of carrots, and then in the future add more based on how the first try works out. With practice you develop a feel for the salt needed for any quantity.

When the curtain raises on the finished dish, I think that exotic, coarse salt gets in the way of the carrots being the stars of the show. If you must add some salt to the finished dish, I'd suggest you sprinkle a small amount of either *fleur de sel* or some pure, flaked finishing salt over the carrots after they have been plated.

If you want, fresh or dried herbs can be added. The leaves of the herbs can either be finely cut and added with the oil, or whole sprigs can be placed over the carrots on the baking sheet. Either way the leaves blacken by the time the carrots are cooked. If whole sprigs are used, many of the leaves fall off the stems and remain on the roast carrots when the stems are discarded at the end of the cooking. With small leaves, such as those found on thyme, this is not a problem. The contrary is the case if whole sprigs of a herb like rosemary are used.

Spices can be mixed with carrots before the oil is added. I'd stick to one or two, and in small amounts. The spices should be ground into their powder form rather than using whole seeds or pieces. Spices that readily come to mind to use with carrots are cumin and coriander. A deeply smoked, Spanish paprika could also be very interesting to use. Even when the spices are mixed with the carrots before the oil they still may form clumps once the oil is added. It's just something you must watch out for and correct if it happens.

With the loose herbs and ground spices, you can judge how much to add in a similar manner to the salt. If after your first pinch and mix, it is hard to see the herb or spice, more may be needed.

Finally, let's roast

The actual process required to roast the carrots is much simpler than it sounds after reading all of the above. After cutting them to shape, place the carrots in a large, wide bowl. Sprinkle some salt and, if you are using them, whatever herbs or spices. How much to use is a matter of experience and personal taste.

Give the combination a thorough mixing with either one hand or by tossing the contents in the bowl. To toss the contents without soiling your hands or another implement, move the bowl upwards so the contents slide up the far side of the bowl and into the air by pulling the bowl sharply towards your body. Then catch everything while moving the bowl outward and under the carrots. That's how the pros do it.

Sprinkle enough oil over the carrot mixture so that they glisten. Start with a little and then toss the carrots as suggested above to mix everything evenly. If the carrots appear a little dry, add some more oil and mix again. If you add too much oil, let the carrots drain in the bowl for a few moments.

Transfer the oiled and seasoned carrots to a plain, rimmed, metal baking sheet. Arrange the carrots in a single layer. If the carrots have flat spots, first line the baking sheet with a silicone-rubber baking mat. I don't like to use greaseproof paper for this application because it moves and tears when the carrots are flipped during cooking. The baking mat has some insulative qualities so the roasting may take longer when it is used.

If you have a convection oven, set it to about 205 °C (400 °F) with the convection fan on. If you have a conventional oven, set it to 220 °C (425 °F). Place the baking sheet with the carrots on a rack near the centre of the oven. If you are using a countertop-style convection oven, place the baking sheet on the bottom rack. It is not necessary to preheat the oven since the carrots are not being cooked 'to the clock'.

The carrots take between fifteen minutes and an hour to cook. You'll know that they are done when the tip of a small knife can easily be inserted into a few of the carrots. Until you become familiar with how the progress of cooking feels, I suggest that you try this first when the carrots are raw and then every ten minutes or so while the carrots cook. As the carrots start to cook, you'll feel the knife tip begin to easily go through the outer area of the carrots, but then come to an uncooked region in the centre. As the carrots cook, the uncooked region shrinks until it is no longer there. Remember that your goal throughout all of this is to test for doneness, not to drive the knife through the carrot like you're plunging a stake into a vampire's heart. Press as lightly as you can with your knife while still trying to advance it.

The carrots need to be turned at least once during the roasting. Until you develop a feel for how long the carrots take to cook in your oven, test and flip them every fifteen to twenty minutes or so. The carrots tend to brown more on their bottoms then their tops, at least they do in my oven. Turning them more frequently evens out the colour but slows down the cooking. I use a fish spatula and a shake of the baking sheet for turning the carrots. Use what you have that works.

When you turn and test the carrots, remove the baking sheet all the way from the oven and close the oven door. Ovens can cool down rapidly when the door is open. This is partially why the carrots take longer to cook if you turn and test too often. All of this gets easier with a bit of practice.

When the carrots are cooked, sprinkle them with a little finishing salt, if that is your intention. I think the carrots are better if served plated. Use your imagination and arrange the carrots on the plate in an attractive manner.

If you are not serving the carrots right away, transfer them to a bowl and cover the bowl with foil. Set the bowl in a place with no drafts and cover it further with a heavy towel. The carrots should stay warm for up to an hour.

If you want to roast the carrots ahead, the cold, cooked carrots can be reheated in a bowl tightly covered with plastic wrap. Set the bowl in a 90 °C (200 °F) oven until the carrots are warm. Alternately, the bowl can

be placed over a pot of simmering water. If the plastic wrap is applied so it doesn't leak, it balloons up when the carrots are warm. It looks cool!

After roasting

The carrots don't have to be served warm. Roast carrots make a very nice salad, especially if the original carrots are small, not pared, and consisting of a variety of colours. Even if the carrots were large and sliced, they still can make a satisfying salad. If necessary, cut the carrots into bite-sized pieces. They may have enough oil on them already, but if you'd like a bit more, add just enough oil to make the carrots glisten lightly. This is a place where nut oils, like walnut or hazelnut oil, work beautifully. A few drops of a mild vinegar heightens the flavour. A little more salt may also be helpful. Trust your ability to taste, but remember to look for subtlety in the flavours.

Closing thoughts

Roasting works well with all root vegetables, but it also works with vegetables like Brussels sprouts, asparagus, and onions. It works less well with vegetables that easily expel lots of water such as tomatoes, peppers, and small squashes where the seeds are not removed prior to cooking. Large, hard squashes are great roasted, but they need to have their seeds removed first and be cut into manageable pieces.

20. Pan-fried Carrots

Although cooks based in modern, English-speaking countries use the term *sauté* to refer to pan-frying, the French word is not used in France to describe this manner of cooking. There is some belief that since the word in French means 'jumped', that the cooking method is referring to having the pan and cooking fat so hot that the food jumps off the surface of the pan when it is applied. This would happen with 'wet' foods where the water would boil instantly when the food is added to the pan, but pan-fried is a broader term than just foods that jump.

Pan-frying is a means of quickly heating the surface of a food added to the pan. Between the food and the hot pan is a thin layer of fat, be it of animal or vegetable origin, that acts to transfer heat from the hot pan to the food. The heat transfer does not rely on the food being in direct and continuous contact with the hot metal. This is good because most food items are not flat enough to make good contact. The surface of the frying pan is usually between 180 and 220 °C (355 and 430 °F). At the upper end of the temperature range, most fats have reached their smoke point and may even have begun to break down. When the cold food item is placed in the pan and thus into the hot fat, the water at and near the surface turns to steam, which is invisible, and vapour, which is what the cook sees. As the steam and vapour are produced, the process makes the sizzling noise we associate with pan-frying. The temperature of the fat is reduced drastically because its heat has been transferred to the surface of the food faster than it can be reheated by the hot pan.

The reduction in heat is only temporary. The fat quickly reheats and continues to transfer heat to the food. If the food is not disturbed, the surface becomes devoid of the water that prevents the surface from increasing in temperature above the water's boiling point. The surface then rapidly rises in temperature until it matches that of the hot fat. As it raises in temperature, the surface browns due to non-enzymatic browning – i.e., browning due to heat, not enzymes as when an apple browns – which we generally consider a flavour improvement. If the surface continues to heat, pyrolysis takes place and the surface blackens and becomes bitter. See 25. Caramelised Carrots (page 118) for a discussion of how to brown the carrots to make them sweeter.

Pan-frying is a cooking method usually reserved for thin objects or food that we only want to cook quickly on the outside. By moving the food rapidly in the hot fat, the temperature rise in the food spreads into the interior volume and the food is less likely to burn. This is the case when we call pan-frying stir-frying.

How much fat?

The amount of fat used in pan-frying is important. Too little and the food sticks; too much and the final product seems oily. My solution is to add enough fat so that it covers about half of the area of the bottom of my frying pan. Sometimes, a little more fat is required part way through the cooking. Usually not.

Pan-frying skinny carrots

Pare and slice your carrots into thin – about 3 mm (⅛ in) thin – shreds or strips (see General Information, page 29). In the food world, these are called a *julienne*, but cooks differ about how thin a *julienne* is. Heat the fat – I like to use foie gras fat, but most people use olive oil – in a frying pan over high heat. When the fat is hot – mine is smoking, yours may just be shimmering – add the carrot pieces. Sprinkle lightly with salt, turn the heat down to a medium setting, and toss the carrots to move them in the pan.

The salt helps the carrots release a little water that turns to steam to further cook them. You want to add salt, but not enough to produce any salt flavour in the carrots. Since this salt must dissolve in order to fulfil its function, avoid using fancy finishing salts. Fine table salt is adequate.

Turn the heat down unless you plan to toss the carrots continuously. At high heat they may burn. Heat is still transferred from the hot pan to the surface of the carrot shreds, but there is more time for that same heat to move into the middle of the shreds and cook them.

Toss the carrots so they cook evenly, and no single surface gets brown before the others. The operative word here is toss. If you just move the carrot shreds along the surface of the frying pan with a spatula or a spoon, only the bottoms are being cooked. You can use a set of tongs or chopsticks to pick up bunches of shreds and turn those before setting them back into the hot pan. Tossing, like you see in restaurants, flips the carrots *en masse*. The process is deceptively simple. If you are using a frying pan with sloped sides, the movement is to sharply pull the handle of the frying pan towards you so the contents slide up the back side and slightly into the air. As the contents are flying upwards, you reverse your move to catch them in the frying pan.

(When I teach students to toss food in a frying pan, we use a small frying pan with some rice or dried beans in it. Also, we practice outside. Most get it very quickly.)

Carrots cook very fast when pan-fried. The easiest way to tell when they are done is to taste them. If the rest of your meal is not quite ready, they will stay warm and not overcook if you cover the frying pan and move it off the heat. If I'm moving it to a cold countertop, I set it on a folded towel to insulate the pan and protect the countertop.

Pan-frying fat carrots

This method works well with carrots that are of uniform size and not too, too fat. Various forms of baby carrots should work well with this method. Larger carrots can be roll-cut (see General Information, page 31) to produce similar-sized pieces.

Start like before by heating some fat in a frying pan over high heat. When the fat is hot, add the carrot pieces. Sprinkle lightly with salt and toss the carrots to coat them with fat. Add enough water to the pan to almost cover the carrots. Leave the heat high enough for the water to boil. Periodically, stir the carrots so they evenly cook. After a while, the water evaporates, and the carrots are cooked. You can tell if they are cooked sufficiently by inserting the tip of a small, sharp knife into a few. If it goes in easily, the carrots are cooked. If there is still a lot of water in the pan, drain it off and add a bit more fat.

If all goes well, the water evaporates leaving the original fat in the pan. With the heat on high, toss the carrot pieces a bit in the hot oil until they start to brown.

If the rest of your meal is not quite ready, transfer the carrots to a bowl, cover with cling film, and keep warm in a very low oven.

When you serve the carrots, sprinkle a little finishing salt over them to bring out all their flavour.

21. Steamed Carrots

If you have the necessary equipment, this is possibly the easiest way to cook carrots. What you'll need is a pot with a lid and a steaming basket.

Of course, some water and carrots are also needed.

If you don't already possess a steaming basket, look for one that stands up straight when not in a pot and that is easy to remove from the pot when the whole basket is enveloped with steam.

Why go to the extra effort to steam when it's just as good as boiling the carrots? If you compare the time to only cook the carrots, boiling is slightly faster. It has to do with the steam condensing on the carrots and cooling them slightly during change of state, but we don't have to worry about that. Steaming is faster for the whole process because there is much less water to bring to a boil, and that's a big timesaver. One disadvantage is that the carrots must be salted after cooking instead of during, which I like better.

Let's get steamed!

The cooking process is quite simple. Add water to your lidded saucepan to a level that almost touches the bottom of the steaming basket. Put the steaming basket into the pot, and arrange the carrots, peeled or not, in the basket. Cover the pot and place it over high heat. When the water boils and steam is pouring out from underneath the lid, lower the heat, but keep a light boil going.

You can tell if the carrots are cooked sufficiently by inserting the tip of a small, sharp knife into a few. If it goes in easily, the carrots are cooked. Remove the steaming basket with the carrots from your pot. If the rest of your meal is not quite ready, transfer the carrots to a bowl, cover with cling film, and keep warm in a very low oven.

When you serve the carrots, sprinkle a little finishing salt over them to bring out all their flavour.

22. Stewed Carrots

The thought of stewed carrots takes me back to the post-war period of the 1950s when stewed and tinned was the most common way to purchase tomatoes. Even if eaten without further cooking, the tomatoes still seemed overcooked.

The method of stewing is a subset of boiling in that the boil is kept to

its lowest possible point of boiling and the food is cooked until soft. The water temperature still needs to be above the 85 °C (185 °F) point where the cellulose that holds the carrot together begins to break down, but not very far.

To stew

Pare your carrots. Either roll cut the carrots (see General Information, page 31) or simply cut them into 5 cm (2 in) long pieces. If the diameters of the carrot pieces are much larger than 2 cm (¾ in) across, slice them lengthwise into two or four wedges. The goal is that the pieces all look about the same size.

Place the carrots in a saucepan. Add enough water to cover the carrot pieces, or at least to float a few. Add a generous amount of salt to the water. It should taste salty like the sea. Place the saucepan over high heat. Watch it carefully. When bubbles start to form around the edge of the water, begin turning the heat control down a little. The water needs to be at the lowest point of boiling where only a few bubbles rise to the surface. As the boiling becomes vigorous, continue to turn the heat control down slightly. As the saucepan material continues to heat up, it only requires the smallest amount of heat to continue the boil at the desired level.

You can tell if the carrots are cooked sufficiently by inserting the tip of a small, sharp knife into a few. If it goes in easily, the carrots are cooked. Drain the saucepan and transfer the carrots to a heated bowl. If the rest of your meal is not quite ready, cover the bowl with cling film and keep warm in a very low oven.

Or not to stew

If the above sounds a bit too bland, consider that there is no stewing constable forcing you to stew only in salted water. The water only serves to transfer heat from your hob and pot to the carrots. Just about any liquid can provide the necessary heat transfer.

Coconut milk fits the definition of any liquid. It works for this, but it may be necessary to dilute it a bit since some brands thicken as they cook.

You could also add other flavours to make the carrots more interesting. A cinnamon stick, a few cloves, a half dozen allspice berries, or even a spoonful of Sichuan peppercorns would all add interest to the dish.

23. Braised Carrots

Should good fortune bring some really fat carrots your way, especially if they are more cylindrical than tapered, choose braising as your method of cooking. Braising is an old method of cooking that combines simmering and steaming and is often reserved for large pieces of tough meat.

The equipment

Braising can be done on your stovetop or in your oven. Any lidded saucepan that is large enough to hold the carrots in a single layer works for the stovetop. If the lid is ovenproof, it would also work in your oven. A baking dish large enough to hold the carrots in a single layer works for oven braising. Since most baking dishes don't have covers, cling film is used to seal in the steam. If your cling film is marked 'microwave safe', it handles the heat of a medium oven.

The braise

Place the carrots in your cooking vessel in a single layer. Add a tablespoon or two of butter or olive oil. Pour in enough boiling water to come part way up the sides of the carrot. Really fat carrots can handle up to 2 cm (¾ in) of depth. Thinner carrots need less. You don't want to submerge the carrots. Salt the carrots a bit and cover.

Place the carrots over low heat on the top of your stove or in a 150 °C (300 °F) oven. The liquid should be maintained at a bare simmer – little bubbles at the perimeter and small occasional bubbles in the centre. It may be necessary to lower the heat after the initial boiling is established.

Even though this method is self-basting, it's probably good to turn the carrots every thirty minutes or so if your cooking vessel has a lid. Cling

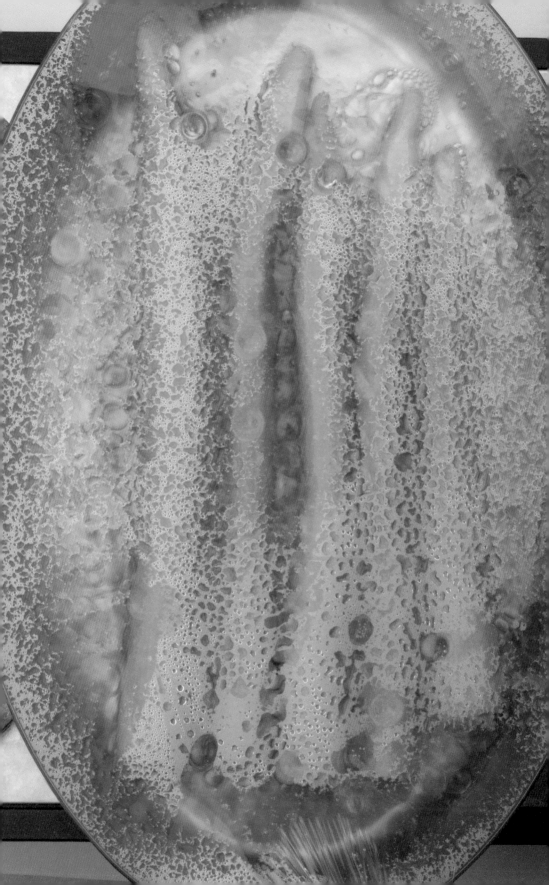

film is difficult to replace once it is removed. If used, shake the baking dish gently to move the carrots around a little.

With the cooking vessel being covered and the heat relatively low, it shouldn't be necessary to add more water. If the original water gets used up, either the heat has been too high, or your covering wasn't airtight. Or maybe your pot has a hole in it?

You can tell if the carrots are cooked sufficiently by inserting the tip of a small, sharp knife into a few. If it goes in easily, the carrots are cooked. Most cling films allow you to puncture it a few times with a small knife without tearing.

To serve

To entertain your guests, you can dust off your grandfather's old carving set and demonstrate your table-side carving ability. Or you can hide in the kitchen and cut the braised carrots into serving pieces out of sight of your guests.

When serving, a sprinkle of some exotic finishing salt may be appreciated.

24. Smoked Carrots

Smoking food is an ancient means of preserving it. In modern times, we are more inclined to smoke food to add flavour. If we only considered smoking carrots to preserve them, then we would use cold smoke so that the carrots remain raw. Here, however, we are interested in both smoking and cooking the carrots at the same time. That calls for hot smoke plus supplemental heat since the carrots must reach 85 °C (185 °F) in order to cook.

There are a variety of devices for smoking, from stove-top versions to large machines, but to smoke carrots a modified grill or barbecue may be best. Many of these can be fitted with a box to hold wood chunks, chips, or sawdust to provide smoke. While the heat from the main fuel source is cooking the carrots, smoke from the smoke box accessory can be generating smoke.

The main items to keep in mind when smoking the carrots are:

- Smoke sticks better to dry objects than wet ones; unpared carrots are therefore better candidates for smoking.

- The early smoke produced by a given piece of wood is less acrid than the smoke produced later; some smokers have a mechanism to change the smoke source when it is half burnt.

- Fat carrots may take too long to cook, and thus be exposed to the smoke for too long.

- Follow the manufacturer's instructions and warnings about how to set up and use their equipment.

I prefer skinny, unpared carrots – just washed and dried – for smoking. As always, you can tell if the carrots are cooked sufficiently by inserting the tip of a small, sharp knife into a few. If it goes in easily, the carrots are cooked. Place the finished carrots on a plate, and cover the plate with cling film. I think smoked carrots are best served cold, maybe with a drizzle of olive oil.

25. Caramelised Carrots

Caramelisation is another example of non-enzymatic browning. Sugar is oxidised resulting in a nutty flavour and brown colour. By weight, carrots are almost 5% sugar, mostly sucrose but with much smaller amounts of glucose and fructose. Fructose caramelises at about 110 °C (230 °F) whereas sucrose and glucose caramelise at 160 °C (320 °F). The trick for caramelising carrots is to bring their surface temperature high enough for the caramelisation to work while not heating it to the point where the sugars break down and become bitter. The trick's secret is to go slow.

Starting out

To caramelise carrots, start out the same as with 20. Pan-fried Carrots (page 107). Do not let the pan go dry. Be sure there is enough fat for

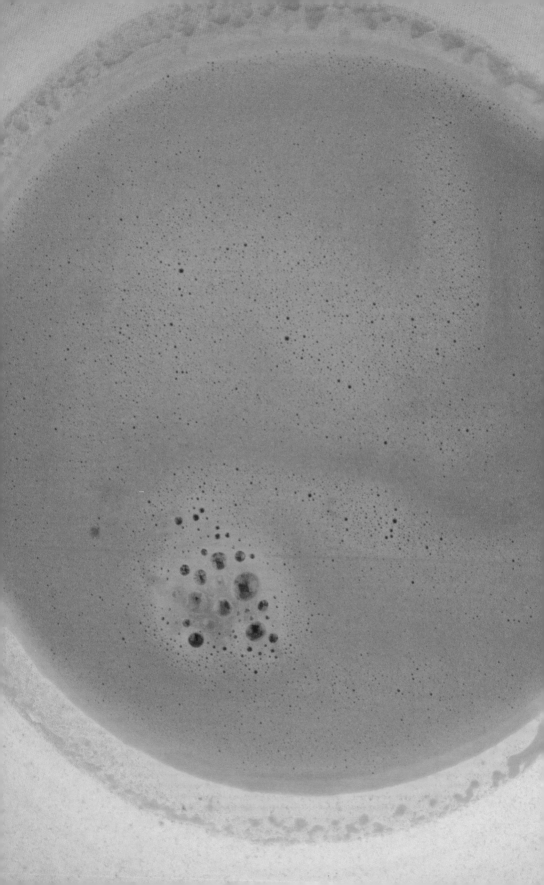

good contact with the bottom surface of the carrots. I prefer a lower temperature smoke-point fat such as butter, but vegetable oils work.

Ending

When you approach the end of the cooking, lower the heat, and continue cooking slowly until the carrots take on a 'brown-around-the-edges' appearance. Thinner areas of the carrots brown before the thicker areas. Just before browning, the surface of the carrots takes on a lighter colour and appears like it is covered with very tiny bubbles. Continue cooking the carrots until about a third of the total surfaces are browned. The carrot pieces or shreds should be getting quite soft so use a lot of care as you toss them around the pan.

When serving, taste for salt. The salt helps bring out the sweetness.

26. Carrot Soup

I have yet to meet a vegetable that can't be turned into soup. Most vegetable-based soups are created from a selection of vegetables. Our goal here is to create a couple of carrot soups consisting mostly of carrots. Both can be embellished or expanded with other ingredients, but is it really necessary?

When making soup, the first thing I consider is the size of my soup bowls. My soup bowls, technically 'soup plates', have a serving capacity of 200 ml (7 fl oz). I prefer to make soup for one night rather than a whole week. The following recipes are proportioned for two servings in my home, but they scale up and down very easily.

Through thick...

The concept of thickening soups with rice goes back at least to the middle of the nineteenth century. At that time, Jules Gouffé discussed using rice and barley as a substitute for bread, the common thickening ingredient for soups going back to medieval times. Gouffé cooked the rice separately until it was very soft and then added it to the soup before puréeing. At the turn of the twentieth century, Auguste Escoffier added the rice to the soup as it was cooking. The soup was then puréed by forcing it through a piece of linen. With modern equipment like a high-speed liquidiser, the whole process becomes very easy.

> 1 tbsp unsalted butter
> 200 g (7 oz) pared carrots cut into 1 cm (⅜ in) thick slices
> 35 g (1 ¼ oz) medium-grain white rice, rice flour, or rice meal –
> not rice starch
> 350 ml (1 ½ cups) chicken or vegetable stock
> 2 tbsp chilled, unsalted butter, diced
> fine salt, to taste

Heat the butter in a saucepan over medium heat. Add the carrots and sweat for a couple of minutes without browning. Add the rice or rice flour and the stock, bring to a boil, reduce heat, cover, and simmer for about thirty minutes or until the carrots are cooked through. As the soup cooks, periodically stir the mixture to prevent it from sticking to the bottom of the saucepan. Continue to reduce heat to only maintain a bare simmer.

Purée the soup in a high-speed liquidiser until very smooth. Return the soup to a clean saucepan. This can be done many hours before serving the soup.

For service, reheat the soup, whisk in the chilled butter and add salt, as desired.

Divide the soup between the appropriate number of soup bowls.

And through thin

Broths are normally very thin soups. This soup can be thought of as a carrot broth where the mouth feel has been enhanced with fat.

> 400 ml (14 fl oz) raw carrot juice
> fine salt
> 2 tbsp chilled, unsalted butter, diced

For service, heat the juice in a saucepan over high heat, stirring often. Season with salt. When close to boiling, remove from the heat and stir in the chilled butter. When combined, froth with an immersion liquidiser. Divide the soup between the appropriate number of soup bowls.

To garnish, or not

The soups above are fine by themselves, but if you want to fancy them up a bit, garnish them with caramelised carrots (see 25. Caramelised Carrots, page 118).

27. Carrot Mash

In modern times, when we think of puréed food, baby food comes to mind. In the days before competent dental care, puréed food also made up some portion of food for the elderly. Later, there's a recipe for puréed carrots as an ingredient in other preparations (see 48. Carrot Purée, page 179), but this recipe produces a side dish as an end result.

To cook

Estimate about 125 g (4½ oz) of pared and trimmed carrots per diner. The carrots only need to be cooked to the point where they are soft enough to purée. Both stewing (22. Stewed Carrots, page 112) and braising (23. Braised Carrots, page 115) are suitable methods for cooking the carrots for puréeing. Cook the carrots to the point that they can easily be crushed with the back side of a dinner fork.

To purée

There are many methods that you can use to purée the cooked carrots. They all produce slightly different results. Be sure to drain the carrots well before puréeing them.

- Use a dinner fork to crush the drained, cooked carrots against the side of the saucepan they were cooked in. After some of the carrots are crushed, combine the crushing motion with a rapid stirring motion. Continue until the carrots are as fine or coarse as you wish. Towards the end, mix in about a tablespoon of soft butter for each serving. Salt to taste.

■ Force the drained, cooked carrots through a food mill fitted with a fine or medium grinding plate. After the puréeing is complete, stir in about one tablespoon of soft butter for each serving. Salt to taste.

■ Force the drained, cooked carrots through a sieve with a fine or medium screen. After the puréeing is complete, stir in about one tablespoon of soft butter for each serving. Salt to taste.

■ Place the drained, cooked carrots in the bowl of a food processor. Process with about one tablespoon of soft butter for each serving. Salt to taste.

Going from dinner fork to food processor, the resulting purées are smoother but also waterier. As the methods increase in their effectiveness, they become more effective in releasing water from the mass.

To finish

Your purée is ready to plate. If you're not, the purée can be kept warm in a low oven, 75 °C (170 °F) or less. Place the purée in a heatproof bowl, smooth the top of the purée with a spatula, and cover the bowl with cling film.

If service is a long time off, wrap the bowl as just described and set it aside. Reheat the purée by placing the whole bowl over a saucepan with 2 to 3 cm (about 1 in) of simmering water. The bowl should sit as far into the saucepan as possible but still be above the water.

When service time arrives, mix the purée again to incorporate any liquid that has escaped.

28. Carrot Fritters

These fritters provide a chance to cook one combination of ingredients using three different methods, and although the ingredient list contains

animal products, gluten, and dairy, with a little cleverness these fritters could be vegan, gluten-free, and/or dairy-free. The quantity of ingredients below produces enough fritters for four side-dish servings.

> 1 large egg, beaten
> 30 ml (2 tbsp) double cream
> 2 tbsps plain flour
> 1 large pinch fine salt
> 200 g (7 oz) trimmed and peeled carrots, grated

Mix together the first four ingredients until very smooth. Add the carrots and mix to incorporate.

You'll probably need to produce these fritters in batches, but they keep warm nicely on a plate at your oven's lowest setting, which is usually around 75 °C (170 °F).

Pan-fry them

Add enough vegetable oil to a nonstick frying pan so that half the bottom of the pan is covered. Place the pan over medium heat. Using a dining teaspoon, not a measuring teaspoon, give the carrot batter a mix, and scoop up a heaping spoonful. Place the spoonful of batter mixture into the hot oil and flatten it with the back of the spoon until it's not much thicker than a piece or two of carrot. You should have several small pancakes in you frying pan. It's best if each is independent and not touching the others.

When the edges start to brown, flip each fritter to cook the opposite side. If the cooking seems too fast, turn the heat down a notch; if too slow, notch the hob up. When brown on both sides, transfer the fritter to a plate lined with kitchen paper. Keep the cooked fritters in a warm oven until serving.

Shallow-fry them

This method is similar to the previous method except that the effect is more like deep-frying. Add vegetable oil to the frying pan until the depth is about 3 mm (⅛ in). Finish cooking like the pan-frying method.

Although these two methods are very similar, this method has the potential to produce crispier edges.

Waffle them

A fun way to prepare fritters is with an electric waffle iron. I use one designed for miniature, 5 cm (2 in) round waffles, but a standard waffle maker works fine. Just preheat the iron the same as for normal waffles. If your iron is not nonstick, squirt the cooking plates with cooking spray. Spoon the carrot mixture onto the bottom plate – it can stand a bit of over filling – close the top and wait. On mine, a light turns green when the waffle (or fritter) is done.

29. Carrots au Gratin

The *au gratin* method of cooking has been around since at least 1755. In *Les Soupers de la Cour*, Menon instructs the cook to finish the tops of the three *au gratin* dishes in the book by browning them in a hot oven. Over the next 250 years, the method changed to mean topped with breadcrumbs and browned in the oven. Or topped with parmesan cheese. Or topped with a combination of breadcrumbs and parmesan cheese. Or topped with a different cheese. Some recipes even add a cream sauce to the body of the dish. I guess, Carrots au Gratin can be just about anything.

Almost conventional

Start by preparing the fork-mashed carrot purée presented earlier (see 27. Carrot Mash, page 123). The quantity suggested in the method would work well in this method. Place the carrot purée in a ceramic 'au gratin' baking dish or divide individual portions between small ramekins or small 'au gratin' dishes. Level the top of each dish. Strew a layer of ground, blanched almonds over the purée.

To heat, place the dish in a 200 °C (390 °F) oven until the purée is hot. If the nuts haven't formed a crust, increase your oven temperature to 230 °C (445 °F), and continue baking until the nuts are dry and a little coloured. Try not to burn the nuts.

Downright unconventional

For each serving, pare and trim carrots to produce four or five pieces, 5 cm (2 in) long. Cut a flat spot on the surface of each carrot so it stays in place without rolling. Cook the carrots by steaming (see 21. Steamed Carrots, page 110) or stewing (22. Stewed Carrots, page 112).

When cooked, arrange groups of four or five cooked carrots side-by-side on a baking sheet. Top with a hefty layer of breadcrumbs made from pumpernickel or other dark, European-style bread. Brown and crisp under a broiler. To serve, carefully transfer each 'raft' of carrots to heated serving plates with a narrow spatula.

30. Carrot Custard

Custards may be the most common formulation in cooking. Many dishes start off as or contain custard without being labelled as such. Traditional ice cream is flavoured, frozen custard. A quiche is a baked custard. Crème anglaise is a custard sauce. Bread pudding is a custard filled with bread. Custards can be sweet or savoury.

When cooked, the egg proteins in custards form a weak gel. The resulting custards can range from thin sauces to thick fillings to solid compositions. Starch-based combinations, such as Bird's Custard, use polysaccharides to form the gel and do not meet the normal definition of a custard since they do not contain eggs.

Typically, the lightest custard uses the proportions of 50 g (1¾ oz) of egg to 200 ml (6¾ fl oz) of liquid. In baked custard, the ratio of eggs to liquid can be increased by four times for a very heavy and solid result.

Minimalist

The simplest form of a custard is no more than a liquid to gel and the gelling agent. In this case the liquid is carrot juice. You can use either raw or filtered juice. The filtered juice produces a clearer result. The gelling agent is a whole egg. The egg needs to be stripped of its chalazae – a small pair of culinary tweezers works well for this task – and very well beaten. One 50 g (1¾ oz) egg is sufficient to gel 160 ml (⅔ cup) of juice. Although not required for the mixture to properly gel, I like to add a pinch of salt to the combination to better bring out the carrot flavour.

As to how much liquid to prepare, I usually measure my custard-cup capacity and work backwards. I have cups with a 60 ml (¼ cup) capacity. Leaving a little room for expansion while cooking, I allow 50 ml for each cup. This means that the one-egg recipe fills four of my custard cups.

Combine the egg and juice, incorporating as few air bubbles as you can. Divide the mixture between the custard cups. Carefully pop any bubbles that float to the top using the back of a small spoon. Stretch a single piece of cling film over the top of each custard cup. Secure the cling film with a small elastic band.

Prepare a water bath for use with a circulator so the level of water comes up even with the liquid in the custard cups. The tops must not be submerged. Preheat the water to 77 °C (170 °F). When it reaches temperature, carefully add the filled custard cups to the circulator bath. Cook for an hour and twenty minutes. Please note that this cooking temperature is chosen because it is just slightly above the range of temperatures where egg proteins gel, but below the temperature where the water in the mixture begins to turn to steam, which would cause bubbles in the final dish. With care, this environment can also be created in a covered saucepan, but it is necessary to closely monitor the temperature for the entire time.

One-by-one lift the custard cups from the water bath. Carefully remove the elastic band and the cling film so the condensation clinging to the film doesn't fall into the custard. This must be done before the cups significantly cool so the cling film isn't sucked down to the surface of the custard when the captured air, which has expanded during cooking, shrinks.

Eat this custard warm for more flavour or let cool for more convenience. To reheat, bring a shallow saucepan of water to a simmer. Remove the pan from the heat, and place the custard cups in the hot, still water for ten to fifteen minutes.

When care is taken, this method produces a very smooth result that's good both hot and cold.

Filled

A more traditional vegetable custard consists of one or more vegetables set in a conventional dairy-egg custard mixture. In this instance, the vegetables are cooked before being baked in the custard long enough for it to set. This whole operation can occur in a baking dish or a tart crust.

This custard is a denser version of the one previously demonstrated. The ratio is closer to 50 g (1¾ oz) of egg to 75 ml (2½ fl oz) of liquid, normally milk or cream or a combination of both. For a stronger carrot flavour, some or all of the dairy can be replaced by raw or filtered carrot juice. A teaspoon of starch can be added to the ratio to improve the structural strength of the custard. Because this custard is filled with vegetables, each corner on a piece of vegetable is another place where the custard may tear. The starch helps to prevent this.

The custard is only intended to fill the spaces between the vegetable pieces. The liquid supports about twice its weight in vegetables. In the previous paragraph, the single-egg custard weighs about 125 g (4⅜ oz) and supports about 250 g (8¾ oz) of vegetables.

How much to make?

You can estimate how much filling is required for your baking dish or tart shell by determining its volume in cubic centimetres. One cubic centimetre is approximately equivalent to one gram of filling. As an example, assume a 28 cm (11 in) round by 2.5 cm (1 in) deep tart pan lined with a 3 mm (⅛ in) thick crust. The space for the filling is approximately

27.5 cm (10¾ in) round by 2 cm (¾ in) high. The volume of the space calculates to about 1200 cm^3 (72 in^3), or large enough for about 1200 g (2⅔ lb) of filling. Since the basic formula produces about 375 g (13¼ oz) of custard and vegetable filling, the tart pan in the example would require three times the basic amount of filling.

Prep the carrots

Cut and cook the carrots by whatever method you prefer. My favourites are shredded and pan-fried (see 20. Pan-fried Carrots, page 107) or shredded and caramelised (see 25. Caramelised Carrots, page 118). Mix the cooked carrots – warm is okay – with the custard mixture. It's best to spoon the mixture into the centre of the baking dish or tart shell, and then use the back of your spoon to spread the mixture to the edges of the mould. It's fine to fill the mould all the way to the top, the custard should skin over during its initial cooking. The skin keeps the custard from escaping. Even so, I always place the mould on a baking sheet to make it easier to handle.

Bake the custard

I tend to bake custards at a higher temperature than most other cooks recommend. I use 205 °C (400 °F) for tart shells and 190 °C (375 °F) for baking dishes. I like my finished custards quite brown on the surface.

Custards, like everything else, bake from the outside in. On the surface, the area near the edges with rise slightly and form a skin while the centre remains quite liquid. If you shake the mould slightly, the centre jiggles while the edge appears stiff. Continue to cook until the centre stops jiggling and the surface is even all the way across. The centre should also feel firm to your touch. If you don't trust your touch, a small knife can be inserted into the mass of the custard near the centre. If there are no 'chunkies' stuck to the blade upon withdrawal, the custard is cooked.

Eat the custard

The dish is too hot to eat right out of the oven. Cooking continues while the mould cools. Cooling helps to firm the custard, so it is less likely to tear when being cut. It's fine to eat the custard when it is still warm, about 10 minutes after it exits the oven.

31. Carrot Spätzle

The Swabian word *spätzle* is the diminutive form of the German word for sparrow. Whoever came up with the relationship between these globs of cooked dough – some people call these dumplings – and birds must have been swimming in one of the local brewery vats. Although my mother was from the next region to the east and ate spätzle as a child, she never served these to me. She did, however, leave me her mother's spätzle maker when she died.

O'ma's spätzle maker consisted of a hopper that slid to-and-fro over a series of holes. The idea was that the dough would fall through the holes into the hot water to quickly cook. When the dough is very loose, these work well. When not, oh well!

When I learned to make spätzle in France, the dough was placed on a board resting on the edge of a pot of boiling water. The cook used a small metal spatula to scrape bits of dough from the mound into the boiling water. With a little practice, a fairly fast pace can be achieved with this method. When the dough is very stiff, this method works well. When not, oh well!

A few years ago, I found an alternative method. The device is nothing more than a sheet of stainless steel that rests on the top of a pot of boiling water. The surface of the sheet is covered with large holes. A mound of dough is placed on the device and a plastic dough scraper is used to move the spätzle dough over the holes. Each time the dough passes over a hole, a little dough drops through it and into the boiling water below. The cook must work quickly because steam from the water heats up the metal and the dough can get cooked into the holes, which greatly slows progress. This system works with almost any consistency of dough. Well, well!

Most families in Southern Germany, Northern Switzerland, and Austria have their own spätzle recipe based around milk, eggs, and flour. To make our carrot spätzle, we'll augment the liquids with lots of carrot purée. The ingredients as listed below will make four small side-dish servings or two large main-dish servings.

150 g (5 ¼ oz) grated carrots
100 ml (3 ⅜ fl oz) whole milk
2 large eggs
¼ tsp ground nutmeg
¼ tsp fine salt
200 g (7 oz) plain flour

Place the grated carrots and the milk into the jar of a high-speed liquidiser. Purée the mixture at your machine's highest speed until very smooth. Add the eggs, nutmeg, and salt. Liquidise to mix. Transfer the liquid to a high-sided mixing bowl. Using a wooden spoon or spatula, gradually mix in the flour. After each addition, rapidly stir to incorporate the flour into a smooth dough. Adjust the amount of flour to match the needs of your spätzle maker. Add up to 50 g (1¾ oz) less for a looser dough, or add up to 50 g (1¾ oz) more for a stiffer dough. When all the flour is incorporated, set the dough aside for a few minutes while the remainder of your equipment is set up and the water is heated.

Bring a large pot of salted water to a boil. Gather the pieces of your spätzle making kit, and do any required assembly. Place a large strainer or colander over a bowl. Have a large slotted spoon or large skimmer at the ready.

When the water comes to a boil, start making your spätzle according to the rules of your maker. Work in batches. When the first batch floats, use the spoon or skimmer to move the cooked spätzle from the pot, pausing over the pot briefly to drain most of the water, to the strainer or colander. Proceed with the remaining batches until all the dough is used.

If you won't be eating it hot out of the pot, move the drained spätzle to a bowl and coat with a little neutral-tasting oil. Refrigerate the spätzle until shortly before reheating for service.

I like my spätzle reheated by browning it in butter in a frying pan over high heat. Other people prefer it like other pastas: with a sauce. Except the sauce is a brown meat sauce, not a tomato sauce.

32. Macaroni & Carrot

When I was a child and later as a college student, I loved the macaroni and cheese that came in the blue box. It was simple to prepare: boil some water, cook the macaroni, drain, mix with butter and milk, and mix in the orange cheese powder. As an adult, one box seems like a proper, single-person portion.

When I first made carrot powder (see 47. Carrot Powder, page 177), it immediately reminded me of the orange-coloured cheese powder in the blue box. So, I quickly created a small test batch. Yes. That was it! And here it is!

The following quantities are about right for a single serving of Macaroni & Carrot when served as a side dish. Doubled, it is adequate for most people as a main course.

> 50 g (1¾ oz) small, elbow macaroni, or similar dried pasta shape
> 30 g (2 tbsp) unsalted butter, at room temperature
> 30 ml (2 tbsp) whole milk, heated
> 8 g (1 tbsp) carrot powder (see 47. Carrot Powder, page 177)

Bring a saucepan of salted water to a boil. Add the macaroni and cook to your desired level of doneness. Drain the macaroni, and return it to the same saucepan. In order, mix in the butter, milk, and carrot powder. Continue to mix until the powder is fully rehydrated. If the mixture has cooled too much, reheat it gently before serving.

Sweet Cooked Methods
Served Cold

33 - 42

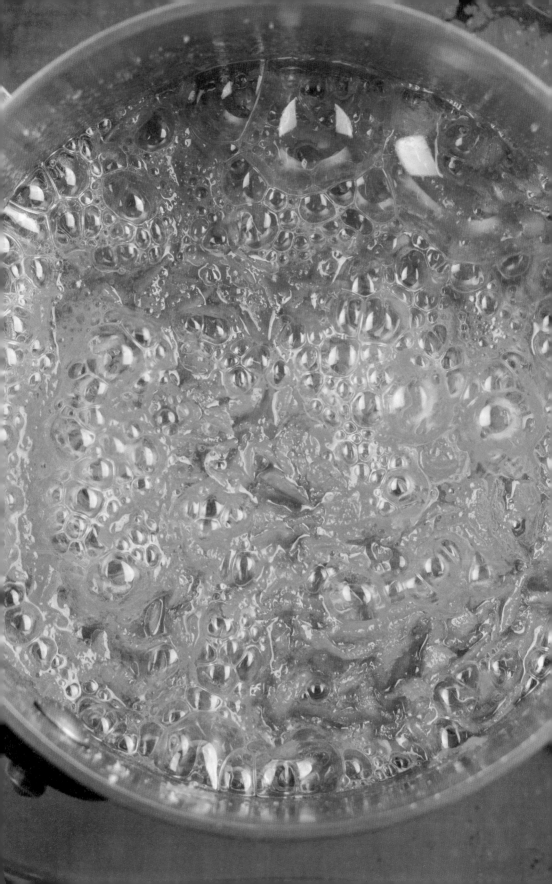

33. Carrot Conserves

In its simplest form, a conserve is nothing more than a foodstuff that been processed with sugar. When I was a kid, our local brand, Mary Ellen Jams, had the slogan: 'a cup to a cup'. They explained that the slogan meant that there was a cup of sugar for every cup of fruit. That has been my jam recipe ever since. As a means of preserving fruit, jams have been around for centuries. Two hundred years ago, most general cookbooks would have a whole section dedicated to preserving fruit in a myriad of methods, but it's not until the last half of the nineteenth century that recipes for carrot jam become common.

The process of making carrot jam is not much different than that for using other ingredients. The pulp of the fruit or vegetable is cooked with sugar until it is hot enough to gel when cooled. By adding some lemon juice, the acidity is increased to help with preservation and to heighten the flavour. Classic recipes also add a bit of alcohol to help with the preservation. If you make the preserve with juice rather than pulp, you'll have jelly. (This is not jelly in the sense of a gelatine dessert, but jelly like quince jelly or redcurrant jelly.)

Carrots are considered high in pectin, the polysaccharide that crosslinks to form the gel that differentiates jams from a simple purée and jelly from a glass of sweetened juice. Carrots also have a bit of calcium which induces the pectin to do its thing when conditions heat up.

The first thing to do when making the jam is to place half a dozen or so metal soupspoons in your refrigerator. I suppose my ancestors used silver spoons, but I settle for stainless steel.

Basic jam

To make a basic jam, you can follow Mary Ellen's slogan and just cook a cup of carrots with a cup of sugar, but you may find that too sweet. The cup-to-a-cup formula assumes a cup of fruit and juice with no air in the measuring glass. If we start with peeled and grated carrots, which is probably the easiest form, the weight of the cup of carrots is only be a little over half (55%) of that of the granulated sugar. I've found that it's best to start with equal weights of sugar and grated carrots.

My preference for sugar when making jam is highly refined white sugar. Pure sucrose, if you will. Less refined sugars contain other flavours that effect the ultimate character and appearance of the jam. If you like those characteristics, use those other sugars.

Grate the carrots using any method you prefer. If you have the patience, an old-fashioned box grater works great if you use the coarsest holes. Most food processors come with some sort of a shredding attachment or two. The coarsest shredding plate available is best for this. I have a shredding attachment for my stand mixer that works great since I can shred directly into a large bowl and don't need to transfer from a food processor bowl multiple times if I'm making lots of jam. The shredding attachment for the mixer is also quicker and easier to clean than the food processor.

Just place the sugar and carrots into a saucepan with a heavy bottom, give the contents a quick mix, and place the pan over a hob on your stove. Start on a medium setting and then when the mixture is boiling nicely, turn the heat down. There's no need to hurry. If you are using a gas hob, it may be difficult to maintain a low enough heat without using some form of heat tamer.

Do not cover the saucepan during the entire process. One of your goals is to evaporate much of the water that is released by the carrots. Do not increase the heat to speed up the process. If you do, you risk burning the sugar and ruining your jam by making it bitter.

During the cooking, stir the soon-to-be-jam with a wooden spoon. The material probably isn't significant, but a wooden spoon or spatula connects us with our ancestors. Any non-reactive material is fine. Early in the cooking, stir every minute or so. As the cooking progresses stir less frequently. As the cooking continues, and the mixture thickens, you can see this happening if you watch the size and frequency of the bubbles. As the viscosity increases, the bubbles decrease in size and seem a bit lazy. That's the time to start monitoring the temperature. The gelling temperature is about 104 °C (220 °F), but the mixture may need to get warmer to produce a nice, gelled jam.

When the jam seems to thicken and it reaches the gelling temperature, which indicates that much of the water has evaporated from the mixture, take one of the spoons from your fridge. Quickly dip it into the hot, bubbling jam and just as quickly lift it out. If the jam comes off the spoon as a sheet rather than drips, it is cooked.

Finish the jam by adding about a tablespoon of lemon juice for each 250 ml (1 cup) of cooked jam. If you want to add the liquor, as they did in the nineteenth century, a tablespoon or so per 250 ml (1 cup) is adequate.

If you've only prepared a small quantity of jam, the contents of your saucepan can simply be transferred to a sealable container. Even though there is probably enough sugar and acid to prevent the jam from spoiling if left on your counter, storage in your refrigerator is probably preferable.

If you've prepared more than a small quantity, it is best to jar the jam. Prepare as many small glass jars with new one- or two-piece lids as are needed. My mother used to boil the jars, lids, and any tools being used for ten minutes. I've always just washed everything in hot, soapy water. I hear that some people just use everything hot out of their dishwasher. If the jars and lids are clean, the jam will probably not spoil. Have your jars and lids ready before the jam is finished. As soon as it is done, place a canning funnel into the first jar and ladle the very hot jam into the jar. Some funnels have a mark to indicate when the jar is filled leaving about a 6 mm (¼ in) air gap, called the headspace, between the jam and the top of the jar. If your funnel lacks these marks, you'll have to estimate the distance. When the jar is full minus the headspace, move your funnel to the next jar. Wipe the lip of the jar with a clean, damp piece of kitchen paper, and screw the lid into place. Screw the lid down firmly but do not over tighten it. The jar is hot and over tightening can damage the rubber seal.

Place the jars on a heatproof surface until they have cooled. As the jars cool and the air in the headspace shrinks, each top should, with a pop, go from being domed outward to domed inward. This assumes you are using metal lids; glass lids don't pop. The last step in canning the jam is to inspect that each jar lid has popped, and no jars have cracked. Once canned and sealed in this manner, each jar should be shelf stable.

I store my jams in a cupboard where they are easy to forget. Eventually, the jam may oxidize, but it still seems fine to eat. Once you open a jar of jam, store it in your refrigerator so you'll be less tempted to snack on spoonfuls of the jam.

More complex jam

If you'd like your carrot jam to have a more complex flavour than just that of carrots, there are many flavourings that you can add at the start of the cooking. Spices such as cinnamon, ginger, cloves, star anise, and nutmeg can be added as whole pieces tied in a small bit of muslin, so they infuse their goodness into the jam. Or, you can add the spices in powdered form towards the end of cooking. By infusing the spices in a bag, the carrot mixture can be tasted while its cooking and the spice bag pulled before the end of cooking if their effect is too strong. Although there are probably proponents of both methods of flavouring, your personal availability of each spice, whether ground or whole, may be a function of how they exist in your cupboard.

Other fruits and vegetables can be added to the carrots in the beginning to make a hybrid-themed jam. I'd avoid green vegetables that may give the jam an unappetizing colour if the ingredient dissolves. Red fruit such as raspberries would make an interesting combination. Likewise, peeled, cored, and seeded tomatoes are worth a try. Green herbs like thyme hold up to cooking and provide an interesting note or two to the finished jam. With a woody herb like thyme, whole sprigs can be added early in the cooking. By the time the jam is cooked, the leaves have separated from the stems and become dispersed in it. Just before canning, the naked stems can be fished from the jam and discarded.

Moving on to chutney

A chutney-style of jam can be made by adding a few additional ingredients to the carrots when the cooking starts. Round onions and moderately hot chilies cut into thin strips can be added. The chili can alternatively be added as dried, small red peppers, either whole or crushed into flakes. Dried fruit such as sultanas, currants,

cranberries, or barberries can also be added. Instead of adding lemon juice and alcohol at the end of the cooking, a tablespoon or two of sherry vinegar per 250 ml (1 cup) of chutney provides the tartness that chutney often possesses.

And then there's jelly

Jelly is traditionally made by extracting a juice from a fruit cooked in water. The cooked fruit is hung in a cloth bag or placed in a cloth-lined colander and set aside to drain overnight. The 'juice' that drains out is then cooked with sugar to the gel temperature. For carrot jelly, you can skip the first step. You can start the jelly with raw juice, filtered juice, or clarified juice. (See 2. Carrot Juice, page 42).

To make the jelly, like before, place half a dozen or so metal soupspoons in your refrigerator. Add a measured amount of juice to a heavy-bottom saucepan. For each 250 ml (1 cup) of juice add 150 g (¾ cup) of granulated sugar and ½ tbsp of lemon juice. Bring the mixture to a boil, reduce heat, and keep the liquid bubbling gently. The gelling temperature is about 104 °C (220 °F), but the mixture may need to get warmer to make a nice jelly.

When the jelly seems to be thickening – you'll see the bubbles become more even and smaller – and the temperature reaches the gelling temperature, which indicates that much of the water has now evaporated from the mixture, take one of the spoons from your fridge. Quickly dip it into the hot, bubbling jelly and just as quickly lift it out. If the jelly comes off the spoon as a sheet rather than drips, it done cooking.

Add alcohol and flavourings in a manner as described earlier. You could even dry the leaves from carrot tops and suspend those in the jelly just before it gels solid.

35. Carrot Macaroons

Coconut macaroons are a common biscuit served during Passover in America. They can also be found year-round in Jewish delicatessens in the north eastern part of the county. Au Petit Délice, an artisan bakery in the old town of Riquewihr in the Alsace, has coconut macaroons as one of their specialties. They are large, but not huge by American standards. If you are lucky when you walk by, there's a plate of sample pieces within easy reach.

Turning carrots into faux coconut

In this preparation, in order to simulate the shredded coconut of the original, it is necessary to remove about three-fourths of the water from the carrots. For the ingredient quantity specified below, it takes about 500 g (1 lb 2 oz) of shredded carrot before drying. Although a food processor would make quick work of the carrots, do this on a box grater so you can make long shreds on the grater's largest holes. By holding the carrot at a slight angle to the grater surface, the length comes out about right.

Dry the carrot shreds on a rimmed baking sheet in a 75 °C (170 °F) oven with the convection fan running. Periodically, run your fingers through the shreds to bring wetter pieces to the surface. They'll look totally dehydrated when three-fourths of their water is gone, but they should still be easy to chew, if a bit leathery.

Turning faux coconut into biscuits

The following quantities produces about 12 to 18 biscuits, depending upon your generosity when spooning out the batter.

> 15 g (1 tbsp) plain flour
> 30 g (2 tbsp) granulated sugar
> dash fine salt
> 0.5 g (⅛ tsp) ground cinnamon (optional)
> 125 g (4 ⅜ oz) dried carrot shreds
> 30 g (2 tbsp) egg white, beaten until frothy, but not opaque

Combine the dry ingredients with the carrot shreds in a bowl and then with the egg white. Set the batter aside for a few minutes and drain off any egg white that gathers at the bottom of the bowl.

Prepare a baking sheet with greaseproof paper or a silicone-rubber baking mat. Preheat your oven to 160 °C (325 °F).

Using a small scoop or a tablespoon, one-by-one, make balls of the carrot mixture that are about 2.5 cm (1 in) round. Space them evenly on the baking sheet. The carrot balls don't expand like normal biscuits, but they may spread a small amount.

Bake the biscuits until slightly browned, about twenty minutes, depending on your oven. Cool by sliding the paper or mat onto a cooling rack.

Cool slightly before snacking.

34. Carrot Meringues

Most recipes for meringues are simply dehydrated sugar and egg whites. Changing either ingredient, both critical, is tricky.

Modern recipes often include a small amount of cream of tartar in order to stabilize the egg whites. In the old days, when egg whites were whipped up in copper bowls, the copper provided the stabilization chemicals. I've never found it necessary to add tartar, even though I beat my egg whites in a stainless-steel bowl. Likewise, salt or vanilla are not necessary in order to produce exceptional but plain meringues.

Most recipes call for adding the sugar a spoonful at a time once the beaten whites become frothy. This is contrary to how I learned to make meringues in Switzerland, where they eat large bars of baked meringue with triple cream.

The quantities below produce about 40 biscuits. The recipe is easily doubled or halved.

Making the meringues

60 g (2 oz), about 2, egg whites
60 g (2 oz) granulated sugar

30 g (1 oz) icing sugar
30 g (1 oz) carrot powder (see 47. Carrot Powder, page 177)

Preheat your oven to 95 °C (200 °F). Prepare a rimmed baking sheet with a silicone-rubber baking mat.

Place the egg whites in a bowl and whisk using a stand mixer set to high speed. When the whites become opaque, slowly add the granulated sugar. Continue whisking until stiff, but not dry, peaks form. Sift the powdered sugar and carrot powder into the whites, and carefully fold by hand to combine.

Place the egg-white mixture into a pastry bag fitted with a 6 mm (¼ in) star tip. Pipe 2.5 cm (1 in) round mounds onto the prepared baking sheet.

Bake the meringues for 2 to 3 hours until dry. Cool before storing.

36. Carrot Cake

It's possible to make a very tasty cake with just three ingredients. You'll use eggs for leavening and to hold the cake together. You'll use sugar for flavour and for moisture retention. Lastly, you'll need something for structure so you'll produce something more than a sweet omelette. Generally, the structural element is flour, but it doesn't have to be. Groundnuts have traditionally been used for structure in flourless cakes. My grandmother used very finely grated, cooked chestnuts for one of her specialties.

To make one of these three-ingredient cakes, the eggs are separated, and the yolks are mixed first with the sugar and then with the nuts or flour. The egg whites are beaten until stiff. The yolk mixture is then folded into the egg-white foam, and the finished batter poured into a cake pan for baking. The combination produces light, moist, and flavourful cakes.

So why not replace the flour or nuts with carrots? Or so I thought. It turned out that the foam wasn't stable enough to make it to the point of being cooked without collapsing into a puddle. The cake looked great, but the bottom was a very wet, baked custard, not cake.

The next thing I tried was to consider the carrots as a secondary ingredient. What if I wanted to add walnuts to a conventional cake? When and how would I do that? Nuts would just be added to the batter before

pouring the batter into the cake pans. So that's what I did with the carrots.

I tried the carrot addition in two very similar recipes. Their biggest difference was how they were cooked: one was baked in the traditional manner, if you're European, and one was steamed in the traditional manner, if you're Chinese.

Western sponge cake

Legend has it that the first sponge cake was prepared for Amadeus VI, the Count of Savoy, in the fourteenth century. That's according to early twentieth-century civil engineer and cookbook author Henri Babinski. The following is based on his recipe.

> 5 large eggs, separated
> 150 g (¾ cup) caster sugar
> ¼ tsp fine salt
> 1 tsp vanilla extract
> 38 g (¼ cup + 1 tsp) plain flour
> 33 g (¼ cup) cornflour
> 300 g (10½) finely grated carrots

Prepare a 23 cm (9 in) springform cake pan by lining it with greaseproof paper. Preheat your oven to 180 °C (350 °F).

Beat the egg whites until stiff. Beat the egg yolks, sugar, salt, and vanilla extract until light and smooth. Slowly beat in the plain flour and cornflour a few tablespoons at a time. Incorporate the carrots. Fold the whites into the yolk mixture.

Pour the completed batter into the prepared cake pan. Bake for twenty-five minutes, or until a knife comes out dry.

Unmould the cake onto a cooling rack.

Eastern sponge cake

In China, where ovens were traditionally not part of a family kitchen, the steamer ably stands in for it. Because of the increase in flour, this cake is not as light as the previous sponge cake. It also lacks a browned crust, but it's also impossible to burn.

> 6 large eggs, separated
> 200 g (1 cup) caster sugar
> 1 tsp almond extract
> ½ tsp fine salt
> ½ tsp baking powder
> 210 g (1½ cup) plain flour
> 300 g (10½) finely grated carrots

Prepare a 23 cm (9 in) springform cake pan by lining it with greaseproof paper. Preheat a large steamer.

Beat the egg whites until fluffy. Add sugar and continue beating until stiff. Beat the egg yolks and almond extract until light and smooth. Fold the yolk mixture into the egg whites. Combine the salt and baking powder with the flour, and then gradually fold the mixture into the batter. Incorporate the carrots.

Pour the completed batter into the prepared cake pan, and steam for thirty minutes, or until a knife comes out dry.

Unmould the cake onto a cooling rack.

37. Carrot Pudding

This pudding is adapted from a recipe I found in Amelia Simmons' *American Cookery*. First published in 1796, the book is generally recognized as the first cookbook written and published in America. It demonstrates an early use of the 'modern' cast-iron oven to bake the pudding instead of boiling it in a buttered pudding cloth.

The quantities listed fit a single 10 cm (4 in) round copper tart pan. This produces four to six *mignardise* servings or a single dessert serving. The recipe easily scales up.

> 75 g (2½) carrot purée (see 48. Carrot Purée, page 179)

15 g (4 tsp) caster sugar
$\frac{1}{16}$ tsp ground cinnamon
15 g (1 tbsp) soft, unsalted butter
1 large egg, well beaten

Preheat oven to 220 °C (430 °F). Heavily butter a 10 cm (4 in) tart pan. Briefly whisk the purée, sugar, and cinnamon together. Add the soft butter and whisk to incorporate. Whisk in the egg. Pour the mixture into the prepared tart pan, and level the surface.

Bake until done in the centre. The edges may start to appear dry.

Serve warm or cold.

38. Carrot Gumdrops

When I was a kid, gumdrops came in two styles. One style was always thimble-shaped and coloured to indicate the flavour. I couldn't tell the difference between flavours as to me they all tasted the same. The other style of gum drops was somewhat shaped like the flavour indicated. Orange gumdrops vaguely looked like an orange section and were orange in colour. Grape gumdrops were purple ellipsoids. Under this style dictate, a carrot gumdrop would have been a dark orange carrot shape. The gumdrops described below are just their natural colour and shaped like micro-shoeboxes.

Initial considerations

Commercially mass-produced gum drops are made in moulds that have unique surfaces that the candy doesn't stick to. In candy shops that make their own, they most likely use cornflour moulds. There are do-it-yourself instructions on the internet for making these at home if you decide to mass-produce your gum drops. I've tried silicone-rubber moulds without success. A small Japanese cake pan that has very square corners and a removable bottom has been my answer, but I struggle mightily to get the finished block of gum drops out of it. Any shallow pan of the appropriate size with a removable bottom should work as well for you.

The quantities given in the ingredient list below produces a 10 to 15 mm (⅜ to ⅝ in) thick block when the base of the mould is about 100 sq cm (15 sq in). You'll need to adjust the ingredient quantities accordingly to match your mould.

Preparing the mould

All the contact surfaces of the mould need to be brushed with a neutral oil. Use a real brush with actual bristles, not one of the silicone-rubber 'brushes' being pushed by vendors for basting hot dishes. Depending on the mould configuration, a single piece of microwave-safe cling film can be adhered to the mould to act as an intermediate surface. You can further push the film into place and smooth it out with the same brush you used for oiling the mould. This deposits a layer of oil on the surface of the cling film, which won't hurt.

The real action

For the mould size described above, you'll need the following quantities:

> 125 ml (½ cup) raw carrot juice, divided
> 10 g (⅓ oz) 225-bloom strength gelatine powder
> 160 g (⅔ cup) granulated sugar
> caster sugar for dusting

Measure out about 50 ml (1½ fl oz) of juice into a small bowl. Sprinkle the gelatine powder over the surface of the juice until it is all absorbed. There is not be enough juice to fully hydrate the gelatine, but the mass should still not be solid.

Place the remaining juice along with the granulated sugar into a deep saucepan over high heat. Bring to a boil, stirring occasionally until the sugar is fully dissolved. Continue boiling until the mixture reaches 115 °C (238 °F). It's fine to turn the heat down a bit if the mixture is still boiling. At the highest heat, it may expand to the point where it overflows your saucepan.

Remove the saucepan from the heat and stir in the gelatine-juice mixture. Continue stirring until all the gelatine is integrated.

Pour the mixture into the prepared mould and set it on a level surface. When cooled to room temperature, move the mould to your refrigerator until fully chilled.

Place a scoopful of caster sugar onto a rimmed baking sheet or rimmed plate. Remove the block of candy from the mould, and coat with sugar. Cut the block into bite-sized pieces, coating the exposed surfaces immediately with sugar. For the cutting, I transfer the block to a cutting board and use a thin knife.

Store the gum drops in your refrigerator in an air-tight container with the sugar separating the individual pieces. Shake the excess sugar from the gum drops before serving them.

39. Carrot Ganache

Ganache can be made out of almost any chocolate, including white chocolate which contains no chocolate. I prefer to use chocolate with a minimum of 70% cocoa mass, which provides a much richer taste in the product than a less intelligent chocolate.

I use chocolate produced for the baking and candy industry that comes in small disks or lozenge shapes. This chocolate doesn't need to be chopped or grated before using. If you start with bar chocolate, you'll need to chop it before weighing.

And thus, we begin

The following is a pretty standard ganache recipe with carrot juice substituted for the cream. Because the juice has no fat, it is supplemented by the addition of butter, which is above 80% fat.

To make about a dozen 'truffles', you'll need the following:

100 g (3½) chocolate, 70% minimum cocoa mass, chopped if needed, see text

30 g (2 tbsp) room-temperature butter

75 ml (2 ½ fl oz) filtered carrot juice
cocoa powder as required

Place the chocolate and room-temperature butter in a heat-proof bowl. Bring the carrot juice to a full boil in a saucepan over high heat. Pour the hot juice over the chocolate and butter. Immediately start stirring the mixture with a wooden spatula or spoon. Continue stirring rapidly until the chocolate and butter are melted and well-incorporated into a smooth mixture. Set aside, uncovered, to cool in your refrigerator.

And thus, we end

Monitor the ganache as it cools. When a spoon scraped across the surface begins to form a ball, remove the bowl from your refrigerator. Place a few spoonfuls of cocoa powder in a bowl. Using a small scoop – mine is about 2.5 cm (1 in) across and holds about a tablespoon – scrape out about a tablespoon of ganache and roll it lightly into a ball. Some cooks wear rubber gloves for this step. I prefer to just work quickly. The balls don't need to be perfect spheres. Real truffles are oddly shaped. Drop the ganache balls directly into the cocoa powder.

When there are three or four ganache balls in the cocoa, roll them around with a spoon until they are well-coated. Transfer the truffles to a plate. When all of the ganache has been turned into truffles, refrigerate the batch in an airtight container.

Alternative endings

Like traditional ganache, this version can easily be used for filled chocolates. It can also be cast into a block and then cut with a wire into rectangular shapes, ready for enrobing or for decorating with a transfer pattern.

The ganache can be flavoured with more than carrot juice. A few drops of bergamot oil will add a citrusy finish, whereas a healthy sprinkle of chipotle pepper powder brings a smoky, spicy character to the finished chocolates.

Besides cocoa powder, peanut flour or similar nut flours also make good coatings. Nut meals, such as almond meal, can be used, but they'll need to be pressed into the surface to get a good coating.

Lastly, a tempered chocolate shell can be added to the raw truffle. The method I learned from one French pastry chef was to place a dab of melted, tempered chocolate into the palm of my rubber-glove covered, non-dominant hand, place a truffle on the chocolate, and to move my hand in a rotary motion until the truffle was covered all over with the hot chocolate. The truffle was then dropped into cocoa powder as before. This produced a thin, hard shell around the truffle. Maybe, instead of cocoa powder, carrot powder should be substituted?

40. Carrot Granita

Granitas are an interesting frozen dessert in that they are best in small quantities. That's in contrast to their cousins the Slurpee, the Italian ice, and shave ice, which are served in larger portions and, in my case, always guaranteed to produce a brain freeze. All consist of frozen, flavoured water except shave ice, which is flavoured, frozen water.

I've worked in restaurants where the granitas are frozen so hard that the poor apprentice cook who has to scrape the surface with a fork ends up bending a few each night. The answer always seemed clear: design your granita so it could be served through a machine. It turns out that if the sugar concentration is below about 15%, the solution freezes solid in an Italian ice machine. If the concentration is above about 30%, the solution won't freeze at all. This recipe shoots for a concentration just shy of 25%, and it has never bent a single fork.

The purest

It works out that adding 25% granulated sugar by weight to filtered carrot juice, which is already just a bit less than 5% sugar, results in it being about 24% sugar. To make about 125 g (4 ⅜ oz) of carrot granita, use 25 g (2 tbsp) of granulated sugar for each 100 ml (3 ⅜ fl oz) of juice. Simply combine the two ingredients in a saucepan and place over high heat. Continuously stir the mixture just until the sugar is dissolved. Pour the liquid into a container suitable for freezing, but leave it on your counter until the liquid is near room temperature. Then cover it, and place in your freezer.

If you serve this granita as a palette cleanser, your portions are small. Use a one-tablespoon scoop to scrap along the surface until the scoop is full. That's one portion. Serve this in a small glass with an equally small spoon. The final product is quite orange when the granita is prepared this way.

The clearest

If you have some of the carrot syrup (see 46. Carrot Syrup, page 174) made by combining filtered carrot juice with an equal amount of granulated sugar, then the syrup can be simply diluted one-to-one with filtered water. The diluted syrup is then frozen.

I serve this granita the same way as the previous one. The flavour of the syrup is a bit nutty from the caramelisation of the sugar, and so is the granita. The carrot flavour is less up front. When served, this granita is almost white.

41. Frozen Carrots

Gelato, ice cream, frozen yogurt, sorbet, ice, and sherbet all have unique characteristics. In my kitchen, ice cream always means frozen, flavoured custard, and sorbet means frozen, sweetened fruit purée. There are a few rule breakers such as champagne and fromage blanc sorbets, but they are rare.

Both recipes below are based on carrot purée (see 48. Carrot Purée, page 179). Each produces a bit more than a cup of frozen desert – enough for four servings. Depending upon how cold your freezer is, it may be necessary to soften these deserts in the refrigerator for thirty minutes or so before serving. Most modern freezers are set to -20 to -18 °C (-5 to 0 °F) whereas ice cream-store freezers are set to -14 to -12 °C (6 to 10 °F) for easy dipping.

If your ice cream machine uses an insert that requires freezing a day in advance, be sure to do this before starting either of these recipes.

Ice cream

> 125 ml (½ cup) carrot purée
> 125 ml (½ cup) double cream
> ½ tsp vanilla extract
> 50 g (1¾) granulated sugar
> 1 large egg

Combine the purée, cream, and vanilla in a saucepan over high heat. Bring the mixture close to a boil. While the liquid is heating whisk the sugar and egg together in a bowl until lightened. When the liquids are hot, slowly whisk them into the sugar-egg mixture. When combined and smooth, return the mixture to the saucepan. Stirring continuously, heat the mixture over medium heat until it begins to thicken and starts to boil.

Set the saucepan in a water-ice bath. Stir the mixture until it is chilled. Freeze the mixture in an ice cream machine. Harden it in your freezer.

Sorbet

> 250 g (8⅞ oz) carrot purée (see 48. Carrot Purée, page 179)
> 25 g (⅞ oz) icing sugar
> 50 g (1¾) simple carrot syrup (see 46. Carrot Syrup, page 174)

Combine the ingredients and chill in a water-ice bath. Stir the mixture until is chilled. Freeze the mixture in an ice cream machine. Harden it in your freezer.

42. Candied Carrots

Over fifty years ago, when I became old enough to drive, one of my first solo trips was the thirty miles from my home to Chinatown in San Francisco. When I got there, I stopped at an outdoor newsstand at Grant and Jackson. I bought a bag of candied ginger and a bag of candied coconut. Then I got back in my car and drove home. My parents never knew where I got the ginger and coconut.

The same technique that was used to candy that ginger can be used to candy carrots. The result won't as spicy as with ginger, but it is more surprising for your guests.

This is one of the few methods for preparing carrots where rounds are the appropriate shape. Choose carrots that, when pared, produce rounds from 2.5 cm (1 in) up to 3.75 cm (1½ in) in diameter. Cut the carrots into thick, 2.5 mm (⅛ in) to 4 mm (¼ in), slices. Whichever thickness you choose, try to be consistent so all the slices cook at the same rate.

Weigh the carrot slices, and then place them in a saucepan. Add an equal weight each of granulated sugar and filtered water to the saucepan. Place the pan on a hob and set the heat to high. By the time the mixture comes to a boil, the sugar is dissolved. Turn the heat down in steps to keep the liquid at a low boil. A few bubbles are all that is necessary. Stir the contents occasionally so all surfaces of the carrot pieces are exposed to the syrup. If the syrup becomes too thick, add a few spoonfuls of hot water. Continue cooking until the carrot pieces are soft and transparent around the edges, somewhere around an hour.

When the carrots are fully candied, sprinkle a layer of granulated sugar on a rimmed baking sheet. Using chopsticks or long cooking tweezers, remove the pieces from the saucepan, one or two at a time, and place them on a bare patch of sugar. Sprinkle additional sugar over the carrots. Using your hands, move the carrot pieces through the sugar until they are separated and well-coated.

Once the pieces are coated, set the whole baking sheet aside to let the carrots dry. Overnight is usually time enough. One note of caution, if you live in a high humidity area, these candied carrots may not dry completely.

Store the dried carrots in an airtight container. They should last a long time if undisturbed, but why make them if they'll be undisturbed?

Methods for Prepared Ingredients

43 - 50

43. Carrot Sauce

There are five ways to categorize sauces: hydrocolloid thickened, protein thickened, reductions, purées, and emulsions. Thickening with a hydrocolloid is the easiest way to make a carrot sauce. Flour and other forms of starch are hydrocolloids. Gums are hydrocolloids. Even agar is a hydrocolloid.

So much for thickeners. But what to thicken? Carrot juice, of course. Carrot juice is not a pure juice. It's a combination of the flavoured water extracted from carrots and lots of small carrot particles suspended in the liquid. If left alone overnight, the juice separates. There'll be a thick line of particles on the base of your container and a thin line of particles floating on top. In the middle with a be a brownish liquid.

Whether to use raw carrot juice or filtered carrot juice for sauces is your decision to make. In most cases, the thickener keeps the particles in suspension, but in some cases, the particles may be perceptible as very small, crunchy fibres.

Thickeners

Flour and starches

Plain flour is a decent thickener for carrot juice. You could start with a standard butter-flour roux, but this is extra work and quite unnecessary. To use flour to thicken, measure out the flour at a rate of about 5% of the weight of the carrot juice – multiply juice weight by 0.05. Whisk the flour into the cold juice in a saucepan. Place the saucepan over high heat and continue whisking gently to keep the flour in suspension. At around 60 °C (140 °F), the starch granules in the flour begin to swell and disassociate. You can stir a lot less from here on because the flour particles are much less likely to fall out of suspension. When the mixture comes to a boil, remove it from the heat. Different flours produce slightly different results.

If you'd like to use a pure starch such as cornflour to thicken your sauce, you should need less than if your use flour. Flour is about 70% starch. Start by weighing your starch at about 3.5% of the weight of the juice – multiply juice weight by 0.035. Different starches produce slightly different results, so test your quantities before making the carrot sauce for an important meal. Starches extracted from grains tend to produce cloudy, duller looking sauces. Starches extracted from roots and tubers tend to produce clearer, brighter looking sauces.

Some starch thickened sauces hold their viscosity for a long time whereas others break fairly fast. Personal testing is helpful. Remember, the quantities specified above are just starting points. If you are not satisfied with how thick your sauce is, adjust the ratio of liquid to starch.

Xanthan gum

This gum is an effective and common thickener and stabilizer. It is produced by fermenting simple sugars. Its name comes from the bacteria *Xanthomonas campestris*, which is used for the fermentation.

Start with raw carrot juice and thicken it with 0.1% xanthan gum by weight – multiply juice weight by 0.001. The gum needs to be sheered into the juice, not simply mixed. To do so, place the juice in a beaker, and stir rapidly with an immersion liquidiser. Slowly sprinkle the xanthan gum over the juice. Continue liquidising until the mixture thickens evenly. Adjust the concentration of the xanthan gum if you'd like the sauce thicker or thinner.

The sauce lasts quite a while in your refrigerator. It can also be heated safely for serving warm.

Agar

Agar is used to produce a fluid gel rather than a standard sauce. As gel implies, a fluid gel is a weakly held structure that flows when it is disturbed. Thus, when you apply a fluid gel to a piece of food with a spoon or squeeze bottle, it flows onto the food, but it then stays in place.

Agar is used in concentrations of 0.25% to 2.5% measured by weight, as described earlier. The low percentage produces a thin fluid gel whereas a high percentage produces a very thick fluid gel. A good place to start is at 1% – multiply the juice weight by 0.01.

In a saucepan, whisk your raw carrot juice with the percentage of agar you would like to use. Continue whisking while bringing the juice to a boil.

The agar should be visibly dissolved. Simmer for three to five minutes, stirring regularly. Pour the agar mixture into a rimmed sheet pan, and let it completely set. Once the gel is set, cube it coarsely, and place it in the jar of a liquidiser. Purée it very briefly to produce the sauce.

This sauce can be heated for serving, but you must be careful to keep the temperature below about 65 °C (150 °F). If the sauce gets too warm, the agar loses its gelling capabilities.

Flavourings

A plain carrot sauce may be your goal, but the sauce can also be flavoured to make it savoury or sweet, or both. Add the flavourings, by taste, to the carrot juice before thickening.

Sweet and sour
For each 200 ml (⅞ cup) of sauce, start with 1 tbsp each of caster sugar and white wine vinegar.

Hot and sour
For each 200 ml (⅞ cup) of sauce, start with ½ tbsp of hot chili sauce and 1 tbsp of white wine vinegar.

Hot and sweet
For each 200 ml (⅞ cup) of sauce, start with ½ tbsp of hot chili sauce and 1 tbsp of caster sugar.

Cinnamon and sweet
For each 200 ml (⅞ cup) of sauce, start with 1 tsp of ground cinnamon and 1 tbsp of caster sugar.

44. Carrot Pesto

Pesto gets its name from the mortar and pestle it was traditionally made with, not from basil, the ingredient used most often in the dish in modern times. So after I purchased my first bunch of carrots with the greens and figured how to clean them, pesto was the first idea that came to mind for their use. Initially I thought about some variations of the ingredients, but I quickly concluded that I should just do a straight substitution of the carrot greens for the basil leaves. I looked at my pile of greens and guessed at how much garlic was appropriate. I put the garlic cloves and a tablespoon or so of pine nuts in the food processor bowl – I don't own a mortar. After these were all stuck to the sides of the bowl and the blade just spun in the air, I added the greens and a pinch of salt. After these were minced and the sides of the bowl scraped down, extra-virgin olive oil was dispensed into the bowl until the mixture started to ball up. The mixture was then transferred to a bowl and an equal volume of finely grated parmesan cheese was folded into it. *Voilà!*

That first batch of carrot-green pesto was used to spread on plain toast. It lasted over a week or so before it was all used. I noticed that during its life, unlike basil pesto, there was almost no oxidation. The colour remained unchanged. The flavour, somewhat dominated by my generous use of garlic, wasn't that much different than basil pesto. It was slightly less aromatic and slightly more bitter.

The second batch was used initially with spaghettini as a sauce. Some of the remainder went in my morning omelette and the rest on my morning toast.

45. Carrot Pasta

In its simplest form, Italian pasta is made from just flour and eggs with a little salt, and Chinese noodle dough is made from flour and water. Neither leaves much room for modification. Either substitute carrots for some of the flour or some of the liquid.

Following the Appian Way

For Italian-style pasta, the pronounced presence of the gluten, a composite of proteins, is very important. Besides being what holds the pasta together, the gluten provides the desired 'tooth'. The question that occurs when you replace some of the flour with carrots is, 'Will the pasta hold together?' If you use a flour that has more protein than is normally used, that may help.

These ingredient quantities produce enough flat pasta for four side portions or two main portions. The results are satisfactory for plated pasta, but not strong enough to produce filled pasta shapes that require folding.

> 50 g (¾ cup) strong flour
> 50 g (¾ cup) carrot powder (see 47. Carrot Powder, page 177)
> 1 large egg
> 1 large pinch fine salt
> filtered water, as required

Place the flour, carrot powder, egg, and salt in the bowl of a food processor. Process briefly to mix everything. Slowly add water until the dough barely starts to come together. Turn the dough out onto a board and form into a flat disc. Wrap tightly in cling film and refrigerate for at least thirty minutes or until ready to use.

The finished dough can be used to make any of the standard hand- or machine-made pasta shapes. There's not enough gluten to extrude the dough and produce smooth edges. It can be used for lasagna, and although it's a bit fragile, it works for simple ravioli shapes.

Following the Silk Road

Since a Chinese-style dough is nothing more than flour and water, it is simple to just substitute carrot juice for the water. Even with the carrot juice, the dough is quite flexible. Besides being usable for noodles, the dough is perfect for dumplings since it starts off as being soft and stretchy. It can be rolled thin for use as wonton wrapper. It is also is excellent for ravioli. The basic recipe quantities shown below produces enough dough for 32 dumplings, 48 wontons, and 4 large bowls of chow mein.

> 280 g (2 cups) plain flour

175 ml (¾ cup) carrot juice

Place the flour in a mixing bowl and place the carrot juice in a saucepan over high heat. When the juice comes to a boil, slowly add it to the flour while mixing with a pair of chopsticks. Continue mixing until the dough barely holds together. Turn your dough out onto a floured board and knead for five minutes or until the dough is very smooth. Cover the dough with a damp towel. Set aside for thirty minutes to allow the gluten to fully develop. Then use as desired.

This dough isn't just for Chinese meals. It can easily be fashioned into most Italian shapes, too.

46. Carrot Syrup

Classically, there are two ways of making syrup: boiling down a naturally sweet juice, and flavouring a juice with sugar. Both can be used with carrots.

Maple syrup is an example of a syrup produced from a naturally sweet juice. Maple juice is about 2% sugar. Boiling down — technically referred to as evaporating — about forty litres of the juice would produce about a litre of syrup. We can use a similar method with carrot juice.

True syrup

Raw carrot juice is about 4% sugar. Clarified juice should have a similar concentration (see 2. Carrot Juice, page 42). If you start with twenty-five litres of clarified juice, the yield should be about a litre of syrup. Once the clarified juice comes to a boil, lower the heat to keep the liquid at a low boil. If overheated, the juice may burn rather than just evaporate. Initially, the pot used should not be more than half full because when first brought to a boil, the liquid bubbles up and may overflow the pot. As the juice is transformed into syrup, the size of the bubbles reduces and their frequency decreases. As the temperature of the syrup exceeds the boiling point of water, the syrup thickens, and the concentration of sugar continues to increase. Stop

cooking the syrup when its temperature reaches 104 °C (219 °F). The syrup developes a slight caramel taste. This caramel taste intensifies if you allow the temperature to increase. You also run the risk of burning the syrup.

This process takes a long time, but you can speed it up. Use a wide, shallow pot. Better yet, use a deep frying pan. The higher the sides of the cooking vessel, the more steam condenses and falls back into the liquid. Cross ventilation helps to get the steam away from the liquid. Remember, the vapour you see is not steam. It's water vapour, which is visible. Steam is a gas, which is invisible.

Simple syrup

The easier method to make carrot syrup is to combine filtered carrot juice (see 2. Carrot Juice, page 42) with an equal amount, by weight, of granulated sugar. This mixture is then slightly boiled to dissolve the sugar. The process can be stopped as soon as the sugar is dissolved, or cooked for a while to caramelise the flavour a bit. Do not cook past 104 °C (219 °F) so the bits of solid carrot in the mixture don't burn. Once cool, the syrup can be further filtered or simply bottled. You'll need to shake the syrup before using to redistribute any carrot pieces suspended in the liquid.

This syrup, because of its high sugar concentration, should be shelf stable and last well past your grandchildren's marriages.

47. Carrot Powder

Carrot powder is made by removing the water from small pieces of carrot and grinding the results into a powder. The best source of small, maybe even tiny, carrot pieces is to salvage the pulp remaining when carrots are juiced. The pulp has already lost half its water and may have been headed to the trash bin.

If carrot pulp is not available, finely shredded carrots will have to do. The finer the shred the better. Small pieces are easier to dehydrate than larger ones. Start by shredding pared carrots in a food processor. When all are shredded, replace the shredding blade with the standard cutting blade. Grind the shreds into small pieces that are as fine as the machine can produce.

It takes lots of patience and stamina to hand shred enough carrots to make a decent amount of powder, but if that is your only source, go for it.

Since there's no water in it, carrot powder should last forever. Carrots are about seven-eighths water. 1 kg (2¼ lb) of carrots should produce 125 g (9 oz) of powder. The actual result is a bit less, since some carrot pieces always stick to the machinery.

There are many ways to dehydrate the carrot pieces, most I don't have access to in my small apartment. If you have a dehydrator, be it mechanical or natural, please use it. I use an oven. Whether you use the carrot pulp from juicing or the carrot paste produced by using a food processor, spread an even layer on a rimmed baking sheet. The sheet can be quite full, but try to not go over the rim. Place the tray in a 75 °C (170 °F) oven and go on a vacation. Depending on how moist the initial carrots are, the drying can take up to half a day. Actually, don't go on vacation; you need check the carrot pulp or paste about once an hour and mix it up a bit. I use a wide fish spatula for the task, but many kitchen tools work, even a spoon.

As the carrot pulp or paste begins to dry out, it becomes looser and more separated. The pulp may dry in clumps that benefit from a little mechanical separation with your stirring tool. When the carrots are fully dry, they lighten in colour. When you run your hand through the mass, it also feels dry.

The dried carrots next need to be run through a rotary coffee or spice grinder. Pass the powder produced by the grinder through your finest strainer. The parts that don't pass through the strainer can be ground again. Unless you have an enormous spice grinder, you'll need to do this process in batches.

Place the carrot powder in an airtight container. I store mine in a closed cupboard, but I doubt if light hurts it. The powder should last as long as needed, as long as it stays dry.

48. Carrot Purée

This version of a carrot purée is meant to be used as an ingredient in other dishes rather than on its own as a side dish (see 14. Carrot Spread, page 80). There are two very different sources of the purée, one being raw carrot juice and the other cooked carrots.

Purée from juice

The source of purée from raw carrot juice (see 2. Carrot Juice, page 42) is the by-product of the process of filtering the raw juice. The orange stuff left behind in the coffee filter can be used as a purée in other dishes. To harvest it, carefully lift the filter with the purée out of the funnel once all the liquid has passed. There'll still be a lot of moisture in the purée. Carefully transfer it to a plate lined with six or eight layers of kitchen paper by flipping the filter over on the dry paper. Set the plate, uncovered, in your refrigerator for a few hours. Modern refrigerators often have a built-in moisture reduction feature that helps to dry the purée a bit.

The purée will never be fully dry, but you don't want it soaking wet. Store the purée in a covered bowl in your fridge. It only lasts a few days unless it's pasteurized, which you can do in a microwave. Pasteurization also cooks it, which softens its flavour.

Purée from cooked carrots

Cook trimmed and pared carrots in simmering water until quite tender. You can tell the carrots are done when they crush easily when pressed with the back of a fork. Drain well. Press the carrots through a fine sieve with a rubber spatula. Collect all the puréed carrot from the sieve and set it on kitchen paper, as above. After a healthy length of time drying in your refrigerator, transfer the purée to a storage container. Since the purée was made from cooked carrots, it should last fine without pasteurization, unless it became contaminated with some bacteria along the way.

49. Carrot Filling

Wrapped and stuffed foods are present in almost every culture on this planet. Whether the wrapping is edible, the filling always is. In some cases, the food item is wrapped so that it can be eaten without needing utensils. Think Cornish pasties. These one-handed meals date back to the thirteenth-century tin mines of Cornwall. Other filled foods require utensils, at least in polite company. Ravioli and wontons being two that come to mind.

Basic filling

Since the basic filling is simply puréed and seasoned carrots, you could start with 27. Carrot Mash (page 123). Or you could prepare caramelised carrots (see 25. Caramelised Carrots, page 118) and purée the results using one of the methods described in 27. Carrot Mash (page 123).

Or you could start from scratch. You'll need 5 g (¼ oz) or more of carrot purée, about a teaspoon's worth, for each item being filled. Wontons typically require a teaspoon while common-sized ravioli require two teaspoons. If you decide you need 100 g (3½ oz) of filling, start with twice that amount of raw carrots to allow for water loss and general sloppiness. Pare and trim your carrots. Cut them into uniform chunks. Fry them in a frying pan over medium heat with lots of butter and a bit of salt until cooked through and a little browned. Butter is better than oil or other fats that do not solidify at room temperature. A stiffer purée is easy to fill with, and the cold butter in it provides stiffness.

Purée the filling with one of the methods described in 27. Carrot Mash (page 123). If the filling seems too watery, add some unseasoned breadcrumbs to absorb the moisture. Chill the filling thoroughly before using.

Savoury filling

For a savoury filling, the carrot purée can be left as is, but why? Ground spices such as cumin, coriander, allspice, or cinnamon and dried herbs such as oregano, thyme, or fenugreek can be added singularly or in combinations.

Sweet filling

For a sweet stuffing, the carrot purée can be augmented with dry sugar in any variety. I'd stay away from syrups because they make the filling harder to work with. Powdered ginger can make the filling sweeter and hotter. Finely diced candied fruits and coarsely ground nuts would also be fun.

Wontons

Even professionals buy factory-made wonton wrappers, so you should too. I do. If you have a choice between thick and thin wrappers, buy the thin, square ones.

There are many ways to stuff and fold the wrappers. All seem different than how I learned forty years ago at my local Chinese restaurant. After placing about a teaspoon of filling on the centre of the square wrapper, slightly wet two contiguous edges and fold the wrapper in half to form a triangle with the 90° corner at the top. All the air must be squeezed from the wonton and the edges pressed firmly to seal them. Dampen one of the bottom corners with a little water. The bottom corners are then brought together to lap each other. When they are brought together, flip one of the corners so the inside of one corner is attached to the inside of the other corner. Place the finished, folded wonton on a board or a plate dusted with a bit of starch to rest until it is cooked. Cover the board with a slightly damp towel so that the wonton skins do not dry out.

Savoury wontons are best boiled and sweet ones are best deep-fried. When boiling, be sure that the water is rapidly boiling and there's lot of it. You don't want it to stop boiling when the wontons are added. They cook fast. If overcooked, they start to fall apart. If any of your wontons fall apart in the boiling water because they weren't sealed well enough, there no way to recover them.

To deep-fry wontons, bring a 5 cm (2 in) depth of neutral vegetable oil to 175 °C (350 °F) in a saucepan. Carefully add the wontons to the hot oil and stir gently to confirm that they are separated. When the wrappers are golden brown, remove the wontons from the oil with a skimmer or slotted spoon. Drain as much oil back into the pot as is reasonable. Drain the wontons on kitchen paper or on a rack set over a baking sheet.

Serve the cooked wontons warm, either dry or with a savoury or sweet sauce as appropriate. You might even try 43. Carrot Sauce (page 169). The sweet, deep-fried wontons are also good doused in powdered sugar.

Ravioli

Although you can make the ravioli dough from scratch, wonton wrappers are much easier. You can use either square or round wrappers but avoid the thick ones for ravioli. Place a single wrapper on your work surface. Place a teaspoon or a little more of savoury filling in the centre and moisten the edge all around with a little water. Place a second wrapper over the first so the edges are aligned. Press all the bubbles out and press the edges to seal the ravioli. They can be cooked this way or, for a little more pizzazz, used a round, fluted cutter that's just slightly smaller than the wrapper to cut a fluted edge on the ravioli. Place the finished ravioli on a board or a plate dusted with a bit of starch to rest until they are cooked. Cover the board with a slightly damp towel so they do not dry out.

To cook, bring a shallow saucepan of water to a boil. Lower heat slightly and place the ravioli in the water. Cook until the dough is done. Drain on a clean dish towel.

Arrange the cooked ravioli on a plate. Brown some butter in a small frying pan and pour it over the ravioli and serve.

50. Carrot Cream

Pastry cream is a starch-strengthened custard used to fill eclairs, profiteroles, and the occasional doughnut. Another common use for pastry cream is to line tart shells for fruit tarts. Since it's a custard, the major ingredients are milk and/or cream, sugar, and eggs. Starch is added to provide stability and stiffness. Vanilla and salt are added to enhance the flavour.

There are many recipes in the wind for pastry cream that call for many unnecessary steps and superfluous ingredients. My experience from teaching the recipe many times: It is one of those methods in the cooking realm that is simple if you relax (and whisk very fast).

The following ingredient quantities produce about 225 ml (1 cup) of pastry cream.

> 170 ml (5¾ fl oz) filtered carrot juice, divided
> 9 g (1 tbsp) cornflour
> 1 large egg yolk
> 25 g (2 tbsp) granulated sugar
> ⅛ tsp fine salt
> ½ tsp vanilla extract

Whisk 50 ml (1½ fl oz) of juice, cornflour, and egg yolk together in a roomy bowl and set aside. Add the remaining 120 ml (4 fl oz) of juice, sugar, salt, and vanilla extract to a saucepan. Place the saucepan over high heat and bring close to a boil. Rapidly whisk a splash of the hot juice mixture into the cold juice mixture. Continue whisking and adding until all the hot mixture is incorporated with the cold mixture. If you stop or slow the whisking before all the ingredients are incorporated you risk scrambling the yolk – so don't stop or slow down.

Return the juice mixture to the saucepan over the same hob. Continue whisking rapidly until the mixture thickens. The mixture most likely will come to a boil as it thickens. When it does, you're done. Stop whisking and pour the pastry cream into a bowl. Place a piece of cling film over the cream so that it sits directly on the surface to prevent a skin from forming.

Carrot custard

Although pastry cream is commonly prepared as a mixture to fill pastries, it is great on its own as a custard. Alfred Bird's nineteenth-century custard powder was flavouring with sugar and a thickener. Mr Bird's custard lacked eggs since he was designing his product for people with egg allergies.

Before serving this pastry cream as custard, give it a quick whisk to loosen it up.

Carrot mousse

Fold 55 ml (¼ cup) of whipping cream whisked to soft peaks into the pastry cream to make a form of mousse. Chill before serving.

Carrot tart

Blind bake a tart shell. I think this works best with 10 cm (4 in) round tart pans rather than larger ones. You can either make a normal tart crust or puff pastry from scratch or purchase a frozen one. In either case, make sure the baked crust has cooled before adding the carrot cream. The carrot cream can be added hot out of the sauce pan or spooned in later after it cools. If added hot, the tart should be refrigerated until the carrot cream is cool. I prefer these tarts plain, but you could top yours with diced, candied carrot (see 42. Candied Carrots, page 163). You could even add fruit. If you do so, brush some heated, strained, and cooled carrot conserve over the fruit to give it a glossy finish. (See 33. Carrot Conserves, page 141.)

Should you find yourself without a favourite tart dough or you're not inclined to purchase one, here's a simple one that is super easy to make. The ingredient quantities listed are sufficient for four 10 cm (4 in) tart pans. The nut flour called for can be from any blanched nut such as almonds, pistachios, filberts, etc.

95 g (3⅓ oz) nut flour
25 g (2 tbsp) caster sugar
140 g (5 oz) plain flour
75 g (5 tbsp) salted butter at room temperature
1 large egg yolk, beaten
½ tsp vanilla extract

Place the flours and sugar in a bowl and briefly mix with a wooden spoon or spatula. Add the butter, yolk, and vanilla extract and mix to thoroughly incorporate. Gather the dough into a flat disc and press together. Wrap the dough in cling film and refrigerate for at least 10 minutes before using.

Preheat your oven to 180 °C (350 °F). Press the dough into the tart pans to an even thickness over the base and sides. Blind bake the tart shells until the edges turn golden, about 15 minutes. Upon removing the shells from the oven, press the centres down flat if they've bubbled up at all. When cool, fill the tart shells as mentioned above.

Index